EL AMERICA'S NEXT VIETNAM? SALVADOR

By

Steffen W. Schmidt

EL SALVADOR

AMERICA'S NEXT VIETNAM?

By
Steffen W. Schmidt

DOCUMENTARY PUBLICATIONS
Salisbury, North Carolina, U. S. A.
1983

Copyright 1983 by Documentary Publications

All rights reserved. Inquiries should be addressed to:

Documentary Publications
Route 12, Box 480
Salisbury, North Carolina, U.S.A. 28144

0-89712-146-5

Printed in the United States of America
10 9 8 7 6 5 4 3 2 1

Photgraphs Courtesy of
Wide World Photos
New York

Dedicated to Hoyt, Kelly and Paul

TABLE OF CONTENTS

Introduction

The crisis in El Salvador is difficult to understand because it requires us to think on at least three different levels. The first and most painful is the level of compassion and abhorrence at the personal, human suffering endured by hundreds of thousands of Salvadorans brutalized by war and torture. On this there is no temporizing. Americans are unalterably opposed to the massacre of entire villages, the murder of nuns and unarmed civilian politicians, and the disappearance and torture of women and children.

The second level at which we are expected to analyze El Salvador is in the evaluation of the domestic political

i

and social situation there. Conflicting interpretations of who
or what is at fault for the deepening violence are cavalierly
tossed out in the press, on television and by the lecture cir-
cuit experts. Is it the deep misery and poverty of the masses?
Is it the greed and selfishness of the ruling upper class? Is it
the shortsightedness of El Salvador's military? Is it, as some
argue, the by-product of change and progress itself which has
unleashed a revolution of rising expectations? Moreover,
the history of El Salyador for Americans begins in 1979 with
the advent of the first so-called "progressive military junta."
What happened between 1500 and 1979, and especially what
was going on in that small country in the 1960s and 1970s,
is by and large a dense fog.

Finally, the third level at which we are expected to evaluate El Salvador is in the realm of international politics. We
are expected to sort out reality from contradictory claims that
it is a textbook case of communist subversion, master-minded
in Moscow, Havana and Managua, Nicaragua, on one hand,
and the counter claims that it's simply a home grown revolution with no international implications on the other. It
is here that Americans are expected to make the hardest
choices because it is argued by many, notably the Reagan
administration, that the security of El Salvador is vital for
American's own national security. A Cuba-type regime in
Central America, so the scenario goes, would cause a chain
reaction affecting most or all governments in that area, and
would eventually threaten both the Panama Canal and Mexico's internal stability and rich oil fields.

I have written *El Salvador. America's Next Vietnam?*
to consider all three levels of this concern. In the course of
doing so, I've marshalled new facts, descriptions, and offered
new insights to help fill in parts of the information gap. I
took pains to interpret, analyze and explain the dynamics
of the Salvadoran crisis. It is, alas, a microcosm of events
taking place in the rest of Central America, and it is sympto-
matic of the political and ideological difficulties experienced

by much of the rest of Latin America.

To me, the events transpiring even today in that little Central American country are like the grinding, awesome movement of the earth's crust, as giant geological plates move about and readjust themselves. Human history itself has been built on such cataclysmic events. The most difficult job for the historian or political scientist analyzing such events is to remain compassionate for the suffering of the tens of thousands caught up in the violence and at the same time maintain a sense of history.

The awful cruelties of Europe's peasant wars, of the American Civil War, the Russian, Mexican and Chinese Revolutions and earlier of the French Revolution stand as testimony to the costs of such change. No less do the two World Wars and the toll they took remind us of the integral part which violence has played in our own heritage.

But I digress.

My intention here is not to offer an apology for brutality. Only an explanation.

I am reminded that Sigmund Freud in a letter to Albert Einstein once observed that "Conflicts of interest between man and man are resolved, in principle, by the recourse to violence." This Hobbesian view of man may not be to everyone's liking, but it represents a thread of human history with great continuity. Mean men in politics have more often than not advocated its use as a political tool, as when Adolf Hitler wrote that "The very first essential for success is a perpetually constant and regular employment of violence.," or when Benito Mussolini spoke of "liberating" and "enslaving" violence; of "moral" and "immoral" violence. But perhaps most instructive is Juan Domingo Perón's call to violence in a 1955 speech. He said, "The order of the day for every Peronist . . . is to answer a violent action with another action still more violent. And when one of our people falls, five of them will fall."

The history of civilized politics is, of course, a struggle against this powerful pull of violent action. It is also the struggle to distinguish between legitimate violence exercised on behalf of just causes and that violence which serves only to oppress and exploit human beings. But therein lies the rub. One person's justifiable violence is another's oppression. To correctly discriminate between the two is the challenge.

I hope we can meet that challenge in the pages which follow.

Finally there is the "Vietnam factor."

In the early 1980s, the analogies with Vietnam have come to rest almost exclusively on three questions: Is the United States going to commit troops or advisors to another foreign country?   Are those troops in danger of being killed?   Will the U.S. then introduce even larger numbers of soldiers into the conflict?   This factor has created an atmosphere both in the U.S. Congress and among the press and public which poses a serious challenge to the future use of force in foreign affairs.   In almost any setting from Beirut, Lebanon, to El Salvador, the question is raised "Will this turn into another Vietnam?

I have attempted to move away from that formula and have pointed out instead the more analytical Vietnam analogies; those dealing with the "regionalization" of conflict, with American policy scenarios, with the domestic issues in El Salvador, as well as addressing the Vietnam questions raised by others in both the United States and El Salvador. I do believe that if the United States was to send troops into El Salvador —an unlikely event— Americans would find themselves in a regionally dangerous and hostile environment not dissimilar to that of Southeast Asia.   In that conclusion, I am in the company of two-thirds of "informed" Americans (those who knew something about U.S. policy in El Salvador) responding to a March 15, 1981 Gallup Poll. When asked, "How likely is it that the situation will become "another Vietnam"? Forty percent said it was likely or very likely. Democrats, independents, and those who had voted for third-party candidate John Anderson in the November 1980 U.S. presidential election were the most fearful of a Vietnam-like entanglement.

Another interesting fact which the poll revealed was that only 63 percent of those sampled could be considered "informed." Thirty-seven percent had not heard or read about El Salvador and did not know which side the United States was supporting.

When the question, "Should the U.S. help the government of El Salvador? " was asked, twenty-eight percent said we should help. twenty-nine percent said we should stay out completely and fifty-five percent did not know. Those who thought the U.S. should help President Jose Napoleon Duarte and the Salvadoran government were asked which type of aid the United States should give. Their answers were:

Economic aid	19 percent
Military supplies	16 percent
Military advisors	18 percent
U.S. troops	2 percent

While it is difficult to estimate the direct impact of American public opinion on U.S. policy in El Salvador, three points are clear: Americans have not been well informed about El Salvador; Americans are influenced by a "Vietnam factor," and Americans are extremely skittish about the use of United States troops.

The combination of these factors probably has a direct impact on how events in El Salvador itself have unfolded. The revolutionary guerrilla groups are quite sure that they will not have to contend with American forces in their struggle to seize control. Right-wing forces in El Salvador have been convinced that they cannot count on the United States to provide direct help, so they have tended to develop strategies designed to go it alone against the revolutionaries (including the creation of "death squads," and para-military organizations). And those opposed to the Duarte government were able to point out that even in the United States only one-third of informed respondents (and far, far less of the total population) favored American help to the then existing Salvadoran regime.

Members of the U.S. Congress have taken notice of the mood among their constituents. This has allowed them, on the one hand, to use their own judgement and vote their conscience so to speak, because a considerable proportion of the voters back home are neither informed nor have an opinion on the El Salvador issue. On the other hand, it has resulted in a very cautious Congressional position concerning U.S. aid. Paralleling the trend of public opinion, economic assistance and some military supplies have been forthcoming, and even a small contingent of U.S. advisors was made available to the Salvadorans. However, even the possibility of sending U.S. troops has been categorically turned down. At the same time, it is safe to say that House and Senate members have not felt either pressure or an opinion trend in their districts and states which would favor a victory by the revolutionary forces in El Salvador.

All this taken together means that the situation is quite fluid. Incidents or events in El Salvador itself, such as the murder of the American nuns or the elections of 1982, will shift the attitude of the general public in the United States. Moreover, as new crises emerge to compete with El Salvador for headlines —the Falkland Islands War and the Lebanese situation come to mind— the White House, Congress and the general public are drawn away from events unfolding in Central America.

The basic premise of *El Salvador. America's Next Vietnam?* is that the pendulum will swing back to Central America and to El Salvador itself. Thus, this book should be a useful contribution to the long-term understanding of events unfolding there.

In the final analysis, U.S. expectations for and U.S. policy towards El Salvador seems to be Ginzberg's theorem at work: You can't win. You can't break even. You can't even quit the game. Perhaps this is true because everyone seems to be playing the game by a different set of rules.

Ames, Iowa
August, 1983

Photographs

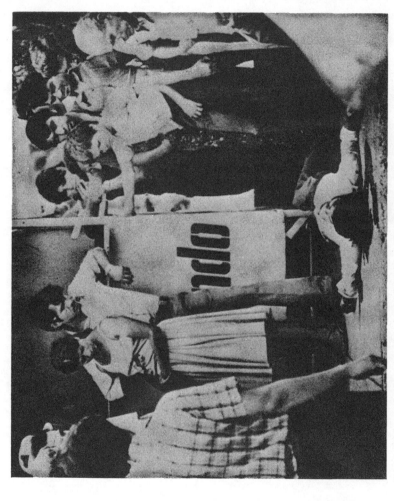

DEATH ON THE STREET. Bystanders crowd around body of an unidentified shooting victim in San Salvador in April 1981.

GUERRILLAS MARCH TO BATTLE. Guerrilla unit pictured on way to fight government troops in northern El Salvador.

PRESIDENT JOSE NAPOLEON DUARTE. Leader of the Centrist Christian Democratic party in El Salvador. Defeated in the 1982 elections.

ROBERTO D'AUBUISSON. Leader of the National Republican Alliance and head of the right wing parties in El Salvador.

LOADING THE BODIES. Salvadoran government troops load bodies of Guerrillas killed near a voting precinct outside San Salvador during the 1982 elections.

JOURNALISTS IN MORGUE. Bodies of four Dutch journalists killed in March 1982. The government denied that the journalists were killed by Salvadoran army troops.

Central America

CARIBBEAN SEA

PACIFIC OCEAN

MEXICO

BELIZE

GUATEMALA

HONDURAS

EL SALVADOR

NICARAGUA

COSTA RICA

PANAMA

1

In the Grip
of Violence

Driving from El Salvador's modern new airport to San Salvador, we turned left and took the long, paved road by La Libertad rather than the new, modern toll road which cuts in half the one hour drive. Dusk was slowly settling in and my driver understated the case. "There is trouble in some of the villages along the new road, especially at night." The two-inch thick bullet-proof glass, neatly built into the specially anti-terrorism retro-fitted Chevy suburban van, removed any doubts I might have had. There was trouble.

Along the darkening road which leads straight and smooth along the Pacific lowlands, hundreds of peasants of all sizes,

sexes, ages, colors and manner of dress were plodding home
from the cotton fields. We passed a brightly lit compound
from which the noise of midway rides, music, the smell of
food and drink, streamed into the balmy evening. I sensed
warmth and security in that community as the farms disappeared behind us. My other companion in the front seat,
pointing his right index finger over his shoulder, said, "One
of the 'intervened' farms from stage one of the land reform."

As the road moved away from the coast, it wound its
way into reddish-brown slashes cut out of hills as if with a sharp
machete. We passed security checkpoints, little country stores,
and small clusters of houses from which warm yellow lights —
candles, weak bulbs, a kitchen wood stove, or kerosene lamps —
reflected along the dark asphalt. I have never liked Latin American country roads at night. In my native Colombia, we avoided
the countryside after dusk. If we did drive to or from our
small *finca,* my father pulled back the slide on his Belgian
Browning .38 pistol, slipping a shell into the chamber. Before
tucking it back into his shoulder holster, under the fading
windbreaker he always wore into the country, he would insert
an extra cartridge into the clip. The one hour drive to San
Salvador that night felt like three. Especially after the houses
and people thinned out. The blackness became intense.
Shadowy forms flashed ahead — trees, stumps, bushes, ravines,
God knows what or who else! A few days later two U.S.
consultants and the head of El Salvador's Land Reform Institute were gunned down at the very coffee shop table where
I had breakfast. Had I known that at the time my clenched
knuckles would have been even whiter.

The next day I observed the burned out shell of the old
San Salvador McDonald's restaurant. Firebombed. It stood in
sharp contrast to the quiet, shaded, lush residential neighborhood. Maids were out early, sweeping sidewalks and watering
plants in the crisp morning air. Weekend plans were being made
for a trip to San Diego on the Pacific Ocean or two days at

Lake Ilopango, 16km west of the city. The noise of excited children packing toys into a jeep, a barking dog, chattering servants readying food for the trip — all drowned out radio news that several civilian political leaders had been abducted the day before. *Diario Latino* covered the opening of a National Tourism Institute two day seminar for industry executives on how to promote Salvadoran hotels, resorts, restaurants and tours; a ridiculous piece of unreality, in a country gripped by violence. On the same page was a story that heavily armed men had burst into the same tourism Institute's headquarters terrorizing employees in their attempt to assassinate a key Institute official. The paper's youth supplement, *Amigos*, carried reports on the quiet and good life: There were color photos of Donna Summer, and features on John Lennon's hit song "Starting Over," the rock group, "The Cars," and the opening of Eduardo Fuentes (the golden voice of El Salvador) at the Riverside Club in a small town called Sonsonate in the eastern part of the country. While the paper reported that a large cache of arms — including an Uzi sub-machine gun, anti-tank grenades, 1,000 rounds of G-3, 300 rounds of 9mm ammo, an MP5 machine gun — was captured from guerrillas in Cabañas province, it also told us that Brooke Shields' and Christopher Atkins' move "Blue Lagoon," was opening at the Caribe Plaza and Terraza Theatres.

El Salvador is a peculiar blend of normalcy and revolution. Its newspapers are loaded with announcements of discount sales, reports on openings of new art exhibits, daily horoscopes, an article lamenting public neglect of the National Theatre (defaced by the smell of swallow droppings which give off an unbearable stench), and the usual international news and sports. Large advertisements extol the value of opening a new savings account at APRISA or the Banco de Credito Popular. I wondered who would be opening savings accounts in a country where in a single day the papers also report a leftist plot to assassinate top government leaders, innumerable attacks against police stations, bombings of buildings, and the machine gunning of buses and where the daily medical examiner's report details deaths by strangulation, gunshot wounds, stabbings and even one poor pedestrian crushed by a bus that was careening overloaded down a crowded thoroughfare. *Por desconcidos* (by unknown persons) is probably the most overworked word in Salvadoran journalism. Parents and spouses daily search the streets for a son or daughter, father or brother who has mysteriously dropped out of sight. A hysterical woman was being consoled on the steps of one agency I passed, another relative victimized by the poisonous fog of secrecy and abduction which hangs over the homes of Salvadorans.

A year ago *desconcidos* attacked the home of Army Colonel Choto. Choto barricaded himself and his family, firing back. An all-night siege began, during which the Colonel and his family resisted until they ran out of ammunition. Finally the attackers firebombed Choto's home, incinerating the Colonel, his family and maid. Their screams rang throughout the neighborhood. How extraordinary that this violence visited one of the upper middle class neighborhoods in a suburb of the capital city. No one came to help, neither government security forces, police, nor neighbors. Thousands of El Salvadorans — farmers, workers, bureaucrats, peasants and middle class persons — have met the same fate. Most offered less resistance than Choto. Who were these attackers: leftist guerrillas, a right wing death squad, the government's own troops, a personal vendetta, robbers? Few ask because asking may be itself a crime punishable by death.

Much of the unrest in El Salvador seems incomprehensible. Why was Concepcion Lopez Angel de Hernandez, age 38, killed by machine gun fire striking the truck in which she was riding? Why did Tranquilino Borja, 35, die the same way in Conjutepequa? A meat vendor at San Marcos market. Dead.

Señora Ana Dolores Castro, murdered by four "subjects" who came there and killed her. Radio repairman Francisco Medrano Chicas was also shot by several persons for "unknown reasons." A shoeshine boy coldbloodedly gunned down in broad daylight on a downtown street, a picture of his crumpled body on the front page. Even more chilling are the constant personal notices pleading for information on friends and loved ones lost in the chaos of civil war.

Salvadoran reality bears little resemblance to life under a stable government. A citizen expects some measure of life, liberty and the pursuit of happiness from his government, trite as it may sound. However, in El Salvador, those who have vanished will never be found. Their families condemned to be haunted forever by the unknown. Their minds tortured by speculations about the grisly and vicious fate of a loved one. I was convinced that a murder victim found in a pool of blood will never be vindicated. The murderer is anonymous; an unknown monster who just fades away. Political decay works daily on El Salvador. "One does not feel like a citizen of a state," one Salvadoran businessman told me. "It's like being all alone and totally vulnerable. Your greatest enemy is other people. All people — any person is likely to be your executioner."

The carelessness of the political actors in this very deadly political game surprises me. Take the event of Thursday, November 28, 1980: at about nine in the morning a group of left and central political leaders began arriving at the Catholic school "Externado San Jose" in San Salvador. It houses a legal aid office run by the church. These men met to plan their strategy to bring an end to the fighting.

Among those at the meeting was Enrique Alvarez, head of the Frente Democratico Revolucionario (FDR), the major co-ordinating group for opposition forces; a tall, fair, aristocratic-looking man, with neatly trimmed hair and an impeccable moustache ("doesn't he look just like David Niven?" an acquaintance noted). Alvarez had been Minister of Agriculture and Livestock in previous administrations. Juan Chacón, leader of the Bloque Popular Revolucionario (BPR), Humberto Mendoza, of the Movimiento Popular de Liberación, Enrique Escobar Barrera from the Movimiento National Revolucionario, Doroteo Hernandez, a less well-known labor leader, Jose Mario Maravilla (BPR) and Leonicio Pichinte of the Ligas Populares 28 de Febrero (LP-28), were also on their way or already at the church center.

Those at the church waited for latecomers, drinking coffee or chatting with a Jesuit Priest named Jose Santamaria, or with the manager of the legal aid center, Br. Boris Martinez. Others exchanged trivialities with the watchman, Jose Abdulio Torres Martinez. Later they agreed to move the meeting to the Metropolitan Cathedral. Some were concerned with security at the center, while others persuasively pointed out that the cathedral had a deep symbolic significance to the people of El Salvador. The violent and tragic funeral of the murdered Archbishop Romero, sniper shootings, burials of murdered political leaders and other past events made the cathedral the touchstone of peace and justice.

Shortly before eleven-thirty an unusually large number of uniformed soldiers appeared on the side streets near the Externado. The soldiers surrounded the school. A red Datsun pickup truck pulled up along the curb by the tall brick wall running along the front of the compound. The driver flicked a half-smoked cigarette out the window and looked in his rear view mirror. A large blue truck drove up, parking by the steel and concrete gate of the school. Fourteen men, armed, wearing a variety of civilian clothes, quickly made their way into the center. Suddenly those at the meeting were rounded up at weapon's point, herded out into the vehicles and whisked away down the Avenida Gustavo Guerrerro — disappearing into the warm, partly overcast morning. The uniformed soldiers faded away.

The next morning I sipped my first cup of coffee and a

glass of *jugo de piña* at the San Salvador Sheraton; what a lovely, peaceful, park-like hotel, built only a few years past to host an international beauty contest. With breakfast I read the newspaper *Diario Latino* featuring a two inch banner headline: "Aparece Cadaver de Alvarez Cordova." (Alvarez Cordova's Body Found). The newspaper carried only fragmentary information. A number of political leaders had been abducted from a meeting and several bodies — showing signs of torture, strangulation, and numerous gunshot wounds — had been found. "My God," I thought, "this is as if John Anderson, Ted Kennedy, George Wallace, Ronald Reagan, Morris Udall, John Connally, Jerry Brown; in fact, most of the flesh and blood of American political leadership, were abducted and killed. It's a disaster! "

I looked around the sparsely occupied coffee shop seeking the opportunity to talk to somebody about this horrifying tragedy. But I couldn't find that vital glance, that reciprocal look which invites conversation. Those who I thought were foreign businessmen or "development experts," were not reading the paper. Most stared with a glazed expression; tired or bored, their eggs were over-easy. Most "development experts" and foreign businessmen never read local papers. Most, in fact, can barely understand the language. The few who can are seldom interested in local news. I once asked a close friend and colleague on a consulting assignment with me in Central America, "Why don't you read the papers? " "I really don't know too much about El Salvador," he replied. Here was a man not mentally in El Salvador. Mentally he was in a 4 x 4 evaluation matrix which represented input into a regional planning project funded by the United Nations. My friend could have been in Ghana, New York, Tegucigalpa, or Zimbabwe —anywhere. He added, "Most places I go, the news is only bad. Human rights violations, poverty, people suffereing. I try to survive, mentally speaking."

My bill paid hastily, breakfast left uneaten, I began a day

of hectic meetings with various government agency persons. The cab driver would not reply to my attempts to talk about the previous day's atrocities. *"Si señor, siempre hay muchos problemas,"* "Yes sir, lots of problems," was the extent of his reaction. When I asked about a building under construction which we passed, he was eager to explain: "That's going to be a very expensive high-rise residency complex, but they built it right in the path of the volcano [which sits silently watching San Salvador]. They say a little underground river runs down from the volcano right under that building. The water is filled with gases from the lava and one day the whole thing will blow up."

The driver dropped me at my first appointment, a government agency which deals with agricultural programs. My destination was a grimy, three-story building at the end of a gravel road in a lower middle class neighborhood. There were the usual little groups of idle men in pants and white shirts hanging about all along the street, sitting on the curb, humped over, discussing little sheets of paper. These are the public employees, hangers-on, seekers of government jobs, relatives, friends.

Violence in the press, the late-night ride from the airport, the cab driver's evasiveness, the kidnappings of the politicians, all suddenly triggered my *malicia.* Latin Americans understand *malicia* and often practice it as a matter of pure and simple survival. *Malicia* is apprehension, suspiciousness, guile, cunning, caution, and hypocrisy. To a non-Latin American *malicia* may seem an exaggeration. But anyone who is Latin American understands to what I am referring. It is a human being's response to total governmental and social chaos. As I slowly walked toward my appointment in the yellowing building, my *malicia* let me figure out where I could dive for cover if shooting started. I chose a nice empty airspace under a staircase. Attempting to pick out the secret police, security informers or death squad boys among groups of loiterers. I settled on two guys with three days' growth of beards—showing an air of confidence in a land where no one has any confidence — they looked around constantly and stared people straight in the eye. I glanced up at the building, trying to see how one would get out of it — perhaps across the rooftops or down a vine — in case a bomb exploded during my appointment. There was no way to get out without returning to the ground floor. And my appointment was in Room 306. There were other problems too: how would I get transportation from there to my next meeting without stumbling or being lured into a death squad taxi, or police interrogation car? I decided it was best to walk, pretending I was a tourist. What tactic should I adopt if kidnapped? "God! I wish I had my dad's Browning .38 in my raincoat pocket. At least I'd have a chance," I thought. "There is not a single person in this whole God-forsaken country who would give a damn if I'm abducted, tortured and killed," was my very frightening conclusion.

This is the kind of thinking that dominates everyone's mind in El Salvador today. It is the mind-set of a theater of disintegration. Perhaps those opposition leaders in school forgot their *malacia;* perhaps Mr. Pichinte was one who did not forget. He was invited, but never arrived.

The next day there was nothing on radio news about the mass murders. San Salvador is not Ames, Iowa or Columbus, Ohio. There is no Today Show on morning TV. At one government agency I located a radio, and began slowly searching the dial.

"Go ahead and try to pick up some news," I was advised.

But no luck. I listened for news, for newsbreaks, for some commentary — anything. But the music and programs were like any other normal quiet day. I did hear a Red Cross public service announcement:

> The Red Cross of El Salvador wants to make
> it clear to the general public and others that
> we are purely a relief agency. None of our
> personnel carry arms. Please respect the hu-
> manitarian effort to help the injured and ag-
> grieved."

A secretary in the office, assiduously filing her nails, asked
indifferently, "Are you looking for something special, sir? "
"I was hoping to get some news on the abductions and
murders of the FDR leaders yesterday."
"Oh," she said, adding almost as if talking to herself, "I
hope they got Pichinte. He's such a horrible person."
Later that day I was in the office of an agricultural expert.
He was an authority on soils. The man was unobtrusive and
shy, U.S. trained, and anxious to please. A phone call
interrupted. The one-sided conversation went:
"When? "
"Did you recognize the voice? "
"My God! "
"I don't want to tell you what to do, but I would go."
"Sure . . . OK . . . Yeah . . . Yeah . . . I understand."
"All right. At five-thirty."
"Don't worry too much. They won't bother you for a few
days. You'll have plenty of time to go."
"My best friend who works at ISTA (The Instituto Sectorial
de Transformación Agraria, in charge of land reform); he got
a phone call this morning at home. They told him to get out
of the country. They would kill all his family."
Tears welled up in his eyes, yet the eyes held me. I felt

helpless. Embarrassed.

"What can he do?" I managed.

"My friend has family in Honduras. He was wondering if he should quit his job. Get out, I told him— Go! If he doesn't they'll kill him.

"Who called? What do they want? " I stupidly countered.

"Who knows. Nobody here knows anything." His reply was complete resignation.

A few weeks later a good friend and high official in the government phoned. My friend is in his late forties, an overweight bachelor who loves above all else his nephews and nieces; a gentle person, trained in England and devoted to the reorganization of his nation's governmental machinery. My friend is a technocrat in the very best sense of the word. He is not a political being, yet has a remarkable sense of loyalty to his country. This bureaucrat with twenty or more years' experience in public service had phoned me from Costa Rica.

"Steffen, I won't be able to complete the project we were working on. I've been targeted. Last week they came to my *finca* and beat up my mother. She's still in a coma. My sister is taking care of her. What can I say? It's the end. I have nothing to do. I'm working in Costa Rica now. El Salvador is dying. And I'm over here."

This atmosphere of uncertainty has tangible effects on the daily operations of the country and the lives of all Salvadorans. Anonymity is prized by many people as a means of escaping violence and retribution. At least if you remain faceless you may not become an attractive target for this group or that. A second side effect of the violence appears in the search for simple escape from the country. There is a brain drain which saps every sector of the educated community. There is also simply a people drain — Salvadorans are leaking, oozing, squirting, leaping and gushing out through every conceivable orifice.

A more basic by-product is that standards of behavior have

become very erratic. Right and wrong become a subjective matter. The most bizarre things are being accepted as a matter of course. The normal process of going to the police or authorities for help seems to have disappeared.

"If the communists invade my factory and destroy my equipment, I will personally see to it that they die," is not an uncommon reaction. On the other hand, people with grievances against the government would never hope to receive redress from another branch of that government as is common in western liberal and stable societies. I am not surprised by the number of non-political people who have gone over to the radical forces, some simply to seek refuge, others hoping to get even for an injustice suffered at the hands of some government agent.

Still another evidence of just how this instability affects the country appears in the massive flight of assets from El Salvador. I was informed that many Salvadorans drove their tractors, cattle, wagons — indeed anything that wasn't nailed down — into Guatemala. All currency is quickly changed into dollars, or any other non-Salvadoran money. Money-changing, in fact, is a complex and quite profitable preoccupation with tens of thousands of Salvadorans. The flight of hard currency from El Salvador is substantial. The assets of many middle and upper Salvadorans now rest in thousands of banks throughout the free world. Gold bars, jewelry, native Indian artifacts, antiques, rare stamps, and even collectible antique cars, are ways of holding onto at least a share of one's life savings. In today's El Salvador, fixed assets such as homes and land can be bought at bargain prices. Such is the value Salvadorans place on their future.

While the wealthy have long been shifting their assets to other lands, in recent times the middle and even the working classes have been caught up by exchange fever. Those with no goods simply drift away with the shirts on their back and a child under each arm. Some of these unfortunate souls end up dying of thirst and exhaustion as far away as the U.S.-Mexican desert border.

A young middle class woman in Colorado told me, 'I'll never be able to live there again. If the communists take over, they don't want people like me back. If the extreme right remains in power, things will continue as they have been. I want to forget where I'm from. It's an embarrassment to be a Salvadoran. I've got to become something else.''

A final observation one hears in El Salvador many times during a day's conversation: "I could deal with a rightist dictatorship, I could live with a socialist revolutionary government; but I cannot live in a condition of disintegration." This is a common view. A moderate government bridging or melding together elements of the left and the right seems remote to most. "Too weak," one person concluded. "The political center is a deserted empty place where only the ghosts of fantasy reside," another person, a young student, concluded rather poetically.

The forces which have converged on Salvadorans and created a sort of hell on earth are complicated. They are also representative of a larger crisis affecting other Central American nations. It would be a mistake to over-simplify the nature of the domestic Salvadoran part of that drama. It would be no less foolish to assume that it is purely a domestic matter. El Salvador is a part of the crisis affecting all of Central America today, and it may be that its solution can be arrived at only by those willing to understand this truth.

2

Domestic, Regional or Global Crisis?

Early in 1978 Americans were treated to the vivid images of Nicaraguan revolutionary violence. These came in full-page color photo stories in the nation's news magazines; the pictures and stories also flashing across network TV screens. A grim young man in a tattered white shirt, his face covered by a woman's stocking mask, was defiantly raising a revolver into the air. The grimy doorway behind him is sprayed with the graffiti of unfamiliar revolutionary slogans. Two Red Cross workers are shown hastily dragging a bullet-riddled body down the sidewalk of a littered street. In sharp contrast stand the neat row upon row of tall, pastel colored doorways receding down the street. The doorways are the only witnesses — silent, colorful — to another wasted human life. Behind the sandbags of a barricade, men crouch in blue jeans, T-shirts and old suit jackets, probably discarded by businessmen, perhaps donated to "the poor," jackets which may have once seen the glitter of fine clubs in Managua, Nicaragua. Each man carries a different weapon; some shotguns, others revolvers, pistols, a steel bar. Here is a ragtag army on a collision course with destiny. But destiny in Nicaragua came before America knew that a crisis was there.

For many years El Salvador, like Nicaragua, held little interest for outsiders. But then in late May of 1979 a large demonstration on the steps of San Salvador's cathedral turned into a screaming, bloody massacre. *Newsweek's* Timothy Nater was in the square when seven Salvadoran policemen began shooting into the crowd. He dove between two parked cars and watched. The nightmare of firing went on for four hours. Dozens died in the bloodbath. Hundreds more were wounded. The blood-soaked, shredded clothes and eerily twisted bodies provided mute testimony that something was very, very wrong in El Salvador. Nater's story concluded that the military started the carnage. He quotes an angry official who had said earlier, "That damn Catholic church. This time they really asked for it," after the demonstrators began throwing Molotov cocktails into the street and firing weapons into the air.

As the world outside became aware of the impending trouble, they were shown red-outlined maps of Central America — that kind of map for which world journalism, and now world TV, is famous. Red arrows pointed to the crisis area. Red stars — looking so much like shells striking targets — pinpointed "recent violence" throughout Central America. One arrow pointed to Guatemala where sixteen had been killed by right-wing vigilantes; another to Nicaragua where guerrillas battled government troops, killing at least 200. A writeup in one news magazine explained that political troubles in Central America were so

polarized that any reformist movement was branded as communist by right-wing governments. More than one correspondent
noted prophetically that such a policy was likely to become
self-fulfilling. And in the weeks that followed, both Central
America and the Caribbean were "re-discovered" by the world
press:

CASTRO: SERPENT IN PARADISE.
MEXICO: BOMB AT THE END OF A FUSE?
NICARAGUA BLINKS IN SHOWDOWN WITH U.S.
PENTAGON'S PLAN: SEND EL SALVADOR MORE
    ADVISORS.
IS EL SALVADOR A DOMINO?
EL SALVADOR: NO VIETNAM?

Not to be outdone by *Newsweek,* in 1978, its competitor,
Time Magazine, carried colored spreads of young insurgents,
masked and armed, battling for control over Nicaragua.
Bloody victims of the furious battles between General
Somoza's national guard and the revolutionaries served notice
that the banana republics of Central America were about
to undergo a dramatic change of mood. By 1979 there were
photos of people huddled Saigon-like in homemade bomb
shelters. In one picture a father in shock, his wife hysterically
weeping, the fiery anger in the eyes of the brother or friend
watching, tenderly carries the blood-streaked corpse of his
young son. It touched American sensibilities. Many Americans
were saying, "Enough!   No more slaughter at the hands of
repressive military dictators." Perhaps the colorful and valiant
if enigmatic rebels could clean up the mess and reform the
system. In July 1979 the Nicaraguan nightmare ended. Somoza
fled the country and the violence subsided. The cold-blooded
shooting of American newsman Bill Stewart by a Nicaraguan

soldier — recorded vividly and endlessly replayed on the United States' television — solidified American public and governmental opinion. An American correspondent had been deliberately slaughtered while doing his job. This single act did much to shift the balance of opinion in Washington. Before long, President Carter determined that further support of the Somoza regime was to end, and it was not long before the Sandinista guerrillas took control. The struggle for Nicaragua was over, at least for the time being. While supported by the Carter administration, this change did not please American conservatives. They viewed the Sandinista guerrilla movement in much the same light as the Castro forces shortly after their victory in Cuba. To them the Sandinistas were communists, and the overthrow of the Somoza dictatorship was but a hollow victory for the democratic forces in the Third World.

The Nicaraguan crisis had hardly subsided before a new opportunity presented itself in Central America. In October 1979, the government of General Romero was overthrown in El Salvador. Experts who follow such events were visibly relieved. Less publicized than Nicaragua, El Salvador suffered from much the same festering sores of secret death squads, government torture and repression, and tens of thousands of ragged peasants eking out a starvation living on small rented farms.

Washington saw in El Salvador an opportunity missed through delay and indecision in Nicaragua. For once, unconfirmed allegations that the C.I.A. had helped engineer the Salvadoran coup proved a boon. Here was America's reply to those who asked why the United States carried out destabilizing covert operations only against "progressive" governments. In El Salvador, it could be argued, the United States had actually helped destroy a repressive government. Moreover El Salvador was bite-sized. In such a small, close-by region it would be possible for Americans to alter the course of events.

From Panama's Darien region to Ciudad Cuauhtemoc in

Guatemala the United States might be able to shift with the winds of reform and nationalism. For the first time the United States was pursuing an enlightened policy in Central America. First came the canal treaties, ceding to Panama complete control over that vital waterway. Costa Rica remained "quiet and safe," while Nicaragua was making a new start. Honduras and Guatemala would not receive U.S. military aid, nor would the Carter administration maintain cordial relations with their governments, until each of those brutal governments altered its policies.

El Salvador too held great promise. A "progressive" new junta had taken power. President Carter was congratulated by liberals throughout the world for having corrected the course and emphasis of United States foreign affairs. Human Rights — that much touted slogan — had become a Washington watchword. Liberal groups throughout the United States could smell victory. This writer remembers the euphoria, a sense of being on the inside, which characterized liberal capitol cheese-and-wine parties in those days. Andrew Young at the United Nations castigated Uganda's Idi Amin, while the Department of State chastized the racists of South Africa. Soon the Shah of Iran too would have the Persian rug pulled out from under him. Relations between the United States and Chile, Argentina, Uruguay and the Central American dictators had never been colder — and that to the liberal establishment was a good thing.

But El Salvador in those days was not quite a national byword. Who outside of a handful of Washington experts had ever heard of such Salvadorans as Ungo, Majano, Carpio, and D'Aubuisson? But the liberals could argue that most Americans have never heard of any foreign leader. After all, foreign policy is not really made or even influenced by the man in the street. Foreign affairs is the domain of that small elite body of professionals which knows how to deal with such matters. If the pundits on the Council on Foreign Relations or in the

Brookings Institution say this is the way to go, it must be right. True, there were obstinate groups of conservatives who complained and obstructed progress. But they had opposed the Panama Canal treaties, they had blocked U.S. foreign aid to the Sandinista government in Nicaragua, and they warned that force rather than human rights would be required to beat back the communist threat in the underdeveloped world.

Naturally the liberal administration and Carter forces disagreed. Why couldn't a middle ground be found? Why not some type of reformism? Why not a gradual opening up of the economic and political structure in these regions? Why not recognize the fact that domestic change in the Third World does not necessarily threaten United States security, nor does it seriously jeopardize vital American global interests?

Certainly it was clear that the American mood towards the end of the 1970s had swung decidedly towards disassociating the United States from the hard-line dictatorships. That, of course, did not mean that the Carter administration endorsed chaos, anarchy, terrorism and instability fomented by any band of subversives or guerrillas. "Nice" opposition and an opportunity for constructive groups to freely organize and press their causes was the ideal towards which liberals aimed. But the liberals and the Carter administration never could differentiate between legitimate struggle and terrorism. Did they realize that time and time again all governments in Latin America — from Cuba to Uruguay — have clamped often draconian lids on dissenters in the name of order and stability? Such was the fate of the Tupamaros, the Montoneros, radical revolutionaries, counter-revolutionaries, liberal student groups, fringe groups, and even single dissenters in Latin American political history. It was naive indeed to believe that in such a climate even peaceful elements struggling for more modest and legitimate change would not meet with the same fate.

El Salvador, unwritten about, unspoken of, and unheard of

by a vast majority of Americans until the early 1980s was to be the testing ground for the new policies of America's liberal enlightenment.

But inside El Salvador a complex brew had been cooking for decades. The classic actors: the military, the fourteen leading families and the revolutionary communist party had been locked in a no-holds-barred struggle for power long before the United States discovered the Salvadoran issue. In addition, there were labor groups, small reformist parties, farmers' organizations, the clergy, student groups of diverse coloration, and a host of other factions, all seeking their rights in a fertile soil of chaos and injustice. Some of El Salvador's political forces indeed shared the American liberal vision of reform. They called for judicial change, fair and open elections, the end of violence, land reform, and an expansion of health, housing and educational programs for El Salvador's people. As one Salvadoran liberal student, now living in exile in California told me, "We sort of hoped to eventually get where Costa Rica is."

But for many Salvadorans the opportunity for reform and change had long passed. To a sizeable right-wing faction, reform was but an open door to Marxism. To others, reform meant a radical change not too far removed from outright revolution, which threatened their jobs, property and rights. The anti-reform faction in El Salvador then did not consist solely of the extreme right, but could count on a sizeable portion of the middle and professional classes in that nation as well.

By the late 1970s, a growing number of politically mobilized El Salvadorans came to view the crisis in their nation as not only domestic, but international as well. Many would argue that the future of El Salvador was tied to the future of the rest of Central America; none discounted the role of Cuba and other left-leaning governments in their support of the Salvadoran communists, and most came to view the United States role as a major causal factor in their predicament.

Mexican journalist Mario Menendez Rodriguez wrote in 1981 that the polarization of classes in El Salvador had reached an "icy coldness," plunging the nation into a profound and irreversible crisis which included social, political, economic, judicial, ideological, cultural and even spiritual conflict. He commented further that El Salvador's elite were to be maintained by the United States, and thus the fate of that nation was controlled by the interests defined and manipulated from Washington. In this context, Menendez saw that the Salvadoran issue was also the Central American issue, the Latin American issue and even the global issue — as seen and altered by U.S. foreign policy. Menendez concluded with the warning, "El Salvador is the strategic piece of the United States in its game of Central American dominos. If it falls, it will drag along with it Guatemala and Honduras. But if the Salvadoran revolutionary movement is defeated in the decisive confrontations of the coming months, then the armed forces of international neo-fascism will intervene in Nicaragua."

Menendez Rodriguez's view of America's role in El Salvador is held by a sizeable proportion of Salvadoran leftists and liberals. Commander Isabel, one of the leaders of the Farabundo Marti Popular Liberation Forces, perhaps the most powerful of the guerrilla groups, said it in no uncertain terms: "The fundamental point in the strategy of confronting imperialism is the Central Americanization of the revolutionary struggle because the United States considers Latin America as its exclusive property in which it can directly intervene when its interests and those of its associates are threatened." Camilo, a member of the same guerrilla organization's National Military Council, added, "The Revolution in Central America is one and indivisible. The Salvadoran process cannot and should not be viewed in isolation or at the margin of what is happening in Guatemala and Honduras."

While all sides concerned with the conflict in El Salvador agree that the abuses and violence should stop, few agree on the ways and means — and even the goals — designed to achieve this end. Even within the United States different groups were reaching vastly different conclusions. Some argued for direct military action, others for political and social reform, while still another group called for a policy of non-intervention. Some saw the dispute as a purely local affair while others tied the El Salvadoran solution to a solution of all of Central America's problems. Throughout Salvadoran society the same dispute holds. Some argue for a military solution; others for social and economic reform. While the extreme right would like to emphasize a local Salvadoran solution, the leftist guerrillas look to link together all their struggles throughout Central America. Only the extreme right and extreme left, it seems, have the solution firmly set in their minds.

As is usually the case, the extreme left is the most vocal and articulate in stating its case. The left sees Salvadoran revolutionary opposition as an integral part of a common fight ". . . to alleviate the plight of the working class masses of our country and Central America." As the Salvadoran guerrilla leader Isabel put it in an interview with the leftist Cuban news agency Prensa Latina, "The powerful struggle in the Central American isthmus, especially in view of the people's triumph in Nicaragua, has transformed all of Central America into a true revolutionary center of action. That is why our organization has as its fundamental point of strategy the Central Americanization of the struggle."

The communist leader Isabel reveals a great deal about her perspective by listing such revolutionary groups as the Poor People's Army in Guatemala, Vanguardia Popular y Socialista in Costa Rica and the "profoundly anti-Imperialist people of Panama" as part of the one force.

Joaquin Villalobos ("Rene Cruz"), Secretary General of the Salvadoran Revolutionary Party and Supreme Commander of its military organization, the Revolutionary Army of the People (ERP), adds that the crunch experienced in El Salvador is found throughout Central America. He explains it as a double crisis: regional as well as peculiar to each country. However, the bottom line, in his view, is the convergence of the capitalist interests of Central America's power base and their control over the armies — the tools with which to defend their riches. He adds what is to become the almost monotonous theme in the rhetoric of the Salvadoran revolution. These oligarchies are aided in their joint defensive interests by the "strategic defense" which American imperialism is projecting in one of the "vital zones for its interests: Central America."

One of the pioneers of the Communist Party of El Salvador (PCS) is Schafik Jorge Handel. He strongly reinforces this view of the close tie between the struggle in his own country and that going on throughout Central America. He goes even further by expressing solidarity with the struggles elsewhere in the world, and emphasizes PCS ties with Cuba and the non-aligned nations.

All the communists in El Salvador see the United States as their principal enemy, and El Salvador as America's next Vietnam. Julia Rodriguez of the National Resistance Party equates U.S. policies and interests in El Salvador with its record during the early stages of the Vietnam War. "That's how it started," she concludes, adding that Guatemala is America's base of operations for Central American counter-revolutionary action. "There, the United States," according to Rodriguez, "is marshalling former members of Somoza's Nicaraguan National Guard, North American C.I.A. agents and adventurers, anti-Castro Cubans, Israeli counter-insurgency experts and troops from the Venezuelan Christian Democratic forces commanded by General Hilarion Carza."

Thus, the scope of factors defining El Salvador's tragedy in the eyes of the left are a function of global forces, manifesting themselves with increasing ferocity in Central America. Opposed to the "freedom fighters" is the international imperialist alliance headed by the United States. In this way Salvadoran Marxists see their struggle as but one part of a global anti-capitalist and anti-imperialist war.

How does this interpretation fit with American perspectives on El Salvador? As previously suggested, Americans are deeply divided on this issue. The conservatives, for example, sound much like Salvadoran Marxists. Both represent two fast-moving locomotives on the same track racing towards each other from opposite poles. *Plain Truth*, a conservative religious publication, voices the conservative view: ". . . with Nicaragua lost," it stated in May 1981, "El Salvador has become the watershed country of Central America."

Gene Hogberg, the author of this conservative article, voices an opinion he would be dismayed to find parallels communist arguments, when he writes "If El Salvador falls . . . the communist tide will be hard to stem. At stake are other Central American dominos — Guatemala, Honduras, Belize, Costa Rica and Panama."

Compare the views of the conservative writer Hogberg with those stated earlier by the communist theoretician Menendez.

Nor is the El Salvadoran right wing's position on Central America much different from that of the communists and American conservatives. In November 1980, El Salvador's *Diario Latino* ran an editorial titled "Honduras is Now the Focal Point of the International Revolution." The editorial argued that with Cuba, Jamaica and Nicaragua "down," the forces of the world revolution need to keep the pace of subversion moving forward. Honduras, penetrated by agents of Nicaragua, would be the most logical target.

El Salvador's *Diario de Hoy* argued much the same point. To that newspaper all of Central America and the Caribbean was to be the target of the communists, just as Laos, Vietnam and Cambodia were at the forefront of the struggle in the 1960s and 1970s. To the editorial writers of the *Diario*, it was not force of arms which defeated the free world in Vietnam so much as it was internal subversion which paralyzed the West's defenses. The *Diario's* writers concluded with the observation that the Vietnam War was "won by the communists on the pages of *The New York Times, The Washington Post, Le Monde,* in the classrooms of Harvard University, and on the campus of Kent State University." It is not without significance that the editorial on this subject in the *Diario de Hoy* was headlined, "We Must Fight for Western Civilization."

The American conservative opinion on El Salvador was probably best expressed by Brigadier General Albion Knight, Retired, Director of the National Security Task Force of the Conservative Caucus, when testifying before the U.S. House Committee on Foreign Affairs: ". . . the main source of trouble in El Salvador is not a relatively small group of left-wing guerrilla fighters," he said, "but the Soviet Union and its American agent provocateur Castro's Cuba." He continued by tying the fate of El Salvador to the rest of Central America, and indeed, to the Third World. General Knight's view was seconded by Colonel Samuel T. Dickens, a consultant to the American Legion. El Salvador, he pointed out, was faced with a serious communist threat. "A fall to Marxist control in El Salvador threatens the stability of the rest of Central America, with Guatemala and Honduras being next." Colonel Dickens concluded by warning that the United States ". . . cannot tolerate a spreading cancer of communism in this hemisphere."

The communists as we have seen hold the same basic views. Only their concepts of the true nature of the enemy differ. The radical communist guerrilla PRN-FARN forces in El Salvador, for example, state that their battle is with "The Pentagon, large multinational corporations and the most reactionary Christian Democrats [of El Salvador] along with the Council for Central American Defense. It is these groups," the radical communists say, "which want to stop the social liberation process of Central America with blood and fire directed against El Salvador and Guatemala, and also against Nicaragua."

So it appears that the domino and integral theory of revolutionary struggle in Central America — and the Third World —

is held generally by both the communists and the right-wing throughout Central America and in the United States. Only American liberals seem unconvinced, and this group appears to hold no single agreed-upon position on this topic.

I am stressing this theme of "Central Americanization" here because without understanding this concept we cannot come to grips with the nature of the complex chess game of Salvadoran internal politics and United States involvement in El Salvador.

In late 1978 and early 1979 the scenario in El Salvador was quickly shifting from internal political struggle waged by an oppressed people in individual nations to a crisis which interlocked a host of actors, spilling over many borders, all tied together by a host of economic and ideological alliances. For instance, it is no longer a secret that Somoza was overthrown in Nicaragua by the acquiescence of Costa Rica which provided a friendly organizational base for anti-Samoza forces. Today anti-Sandinista groups are seeking a sanctuary in Costa Rica, and are openly operating from bases in Honduras.

Salvador Cayetano Carpio, leader of the Farabundo Marti group in El Salvador, revealed in 1981 that a brigade of his forces had fought alongside the Sandinistas, at the same time listing the names of volunteers who had been killed during the anti-Samoza campaign.

By May 1981, the troubles in Central America had reached such proportions that they were the subject of increased press coverage within the United States. The *Christian Science Monitor* that month printed a 36-page special pullout section titled, "Central America in Turmoil." The newspaper's Latin American editor, Jim Goodsell and his staff detailed in a country-by-country analysis the problems affecting the region. By this time all Central America had become, in the words of U.S. Secretary of State Alexander Haig, a victim of regional revolutionaries who misled and used domestic freedom fighters. All nations in that region, Haig warned, were on the Soviet

Union's 'hit list'." In Haig's view Nicaragua had come first, then El Salvador would fall, followed by Honduras and finally—"the grand prize"—Guatemala. Robert Leiken of Georgetown University argued that the Soviets wanted to divert U.S. military resources away from other areas of the world to Central America. And Daniel Sutherland reported that a Latin American newspaper editor had recently accused the Americans of seeking revenge for past failures, saying, "You are going into El Salvador in order to take revenge for Vietnam."

All this attention and speculation about the global significance of El Salvador magnified the dimensions of the problem greatly. If, indeed, the troubles were either instigated by the United States to keep its strategic hegemony, or by the Russians to enhance theirs, the significance of little El Salvador had grown far beyond its traditional place in the hemisphere.

The famous State Department White Paper on Communist Interference in El Salvador issued in February of 1981 added fuel to the fire. Though questions about the authenticity of much of the document have been raised, its impact was certainly massive. Every American newspaper, radio and TV news program carried the story. And indeed it appears that Salvadoran guerrillas were traveling to Moscow, Hanoi, Havana, Prague, Pyongyang and other communist capitals with shopping lists for weapons. W. Scott Thompson of the Fletcher Law School in a *Foreign Policy* article cites Vladimir, a Salvadoran guerrilla, as saying that this is the first Latin American revolution directly assisted by communist powers even while the rebels are still fighting in the mountains and streets. Central America had come of age. It was moving center stage at a critical juncture in global security politics. Even scholars, usually slow to seize upon the urgent events, responded. A series of six interesting articles in the Summer 1981 issue of *Foreign Policy*, analyzed the "Struggle in Central America." Most of these articles stressed that the global perspective exaggerated the outside role in what are really struggles against internal injustice. But the paper by Thompson strongly argued that El Salvador is, at least indirectly, a consequence of the U.S. failure in Vietnam. He recommended that "El Salvador is the place to take a stand against further spreading of Soviet-Cuban influence within the U.S. security sphere."

A *Christian Science Monitor* editorial on July 18, 1980 perfectly summarizes the confusing conundrum in which Americans found themselves as the opening salvoes of the Central American cannons began to reverberate. The editors note that the Carter administration (about to be ushered out by Reagan) had finally decided to address the problem by not simply "looking for new oligarchs to restore the old order," instead hoping that ". . . broader foundations of social and economic justice would produce a new stability." The editorial continues by pointing out that nostalgia for the old ways has led Latin oligarchs and U.S. Congressional conservatives to sap the Carter policies of their juices, the latter by refusing aid to leftists in Nicaragua and by trying to disassociate the U.S. from "the forces of reform" in El Salvador. The editorial concludes that "Whatever the result of our election, the upheaval in Central America will not end soon. To deny that reality is to forfeit a real opportunity — to preserve American influence and to use it constructively."

The *Monitor* was certainly correct in one respect — the upheaval has not gone away. It has exploded into dimensions undreamed of in the summer of 1980. However, it is curious to note that the editorial advocated "preserving American influence" in the region, precisely the factor which most forces of reform in Central America, but most explicitly in El Salvador, have identified as one of the root causes of the problem. One is left to wonder then with which of the many forces — most of them revolutionaly and not reformist — the *Monitor* would build a new U.S. alliance? There is an uneasy inconsistency — really a confusion — about what the precise dimensions of the upheaval are, and as to just how the United States fits into these, either as a healing constructive force or as an exacerbator of the crisis.

This confusion is the theme of a useful article which appeared in 1981. Leonel Gomez, a former advisor to El Salvador's Director of Land Reform, and Bruce Cameron, Special Assistant to Iowa Congressman Tom Harkin, an outspoken critic of U.S. policy in El Salvador, wrote, ". . . that myths and half truths held by American liberals and conservatives alike have colored our views of the crisis."

Among the five "Popular misconceptions" they cite, however, we find only references to Salvadoran domestic, political and economic problems. Neither the extreme left nor the extreme right hold this view. And both these groups are probably closer to the truth, if for the wrong reasons. The simple fact is that the struggle there has been and perhaps always was an international and regional crisis, subject to widely divergent and radically conflicting interpretations. It is a crisis involving everyone from Sandinistas to the Pentagon; from Israel to Venezuela; from secret right-wing societies with "branch offices" in every Central American capital to fraternal revolutionary coalitions spanning the globe; from the ghosts of old Vietnam mercenaries to Soviet experts on revolutionary violence; and from Argentine counter-insurgency officers to German terrorists and anti-U.S. and anti-nuclear factions.

We must approach any conclusions about El Salvador with care. Long standing historical traumas which El Salvador has inherited as part of its historical experience must be sorted out from current regional and international pressures; ideological contortions should be separated from such basic structural problems as hunger and poverty; and simplistic solutions from complex interrelated causes. And these problems are not unique to any one group, either of the extreme right or left. All have their own myths. Some, as we have seen, have the same myths, adopted for different reasons. But for whatever reason, myths do not lead to solutions, only to further confusion and failure.

Above all, recent events in El Salvador have forced upon many a deep burden of sympathy with the human bodies and souls battered about in the furious storm of change. I am personally haunted by the image of a partially decapitated body I saw one day lying by the side of the road outside San Salvador. The face was slightly turned toward me, looking up, eyes open, mouth expressionless. Was this a hardened terrorist on a mission to bomb the Ministry of Agriculture? Was this man caught by vigilant security forces? Perhaps he had resisted, shooting at one of the young peasant soldiers, permanently crippling him with a round in the spine. Maybe the young soldier lies, paraplegic, in an army hospital at this moment, his mother and sister weeping beside his bed. Then, in a fury of retribution, the unlucky rebel was shot on the spot. Or was he simply one of thousands of innocent victims? Perhaps on an errand for his mother. I have no idea who he was or why he lost his life. And that is what bothers me. All the dead in this war and in all the wars in Central America today who die for reasons unknown, with their names unknown, frequently to be buried in unmarked and shallow graves — lost forever to their friends, relatives, and to all mankind.

Salvadorans today are caught in a meat grinder of history. These people are no different from the reader of this book. Given different circumstances, an accident of birth, we all could be caught up in the violent time warp of El Salvador. But the vivid tragedy makes it that much harder to step back and try to analyze what is really going on, who is responsible, and why all this is happening to our fellow human beings.

Yet when one looks at the problem in El Salvador as a regional or global issue, then the perspective changes. It then assumes the stature of an issue — dehumanized if you will — between conservative and liberal; between democracy and communism. This is surely one way to consider the El Salvador struggle. But it is not the way in which full truths will be found. In succeeding chapters we will explore the political history of El Salvador — certainly one of the prime causes of today's crisis, for there is a thread of continuity between past and present which affects the course of current events. We will also look at the key structural factors which made this land of Spaniards, dictators and wizards a place of high drama in the 1980s.

3

Spaniards, Dictators, and Wizards: 1524-1944

San Salvador in the early years of the twentieth century was in many respects a genteel city, reminiscent of colonial Pnompenh, Saigon and other Third World capitals. Its citizens liked to think of themselves as citizens of a small Paris. Men and women imitated the fashions in Europe's great cities. Merchants, professionals, magistrates and politicians accompanied by gracious ladies strolled through the parks at dusk in their Stetson and Borsalino hats. On Sunday mornings, elegant cafes such as the L'on D'or and La Maison Doreé, were crowded. The latest European music was played and maestro Flavio Pineda treated all customers to the lovely strains of

32

waltzes and minuets, often accompanied by the accomplished violins of the Navarro brothers.

Glass after glass of Martell No. 4 cognac, wine and sangria washed down dainty pastries and lovingly prepared canapés. Some stopped their promenade long enough to savor a fruit drink at La Gran Via, a popular restaurant located at El Portal, between the sangria store and Almacen La Dalia. Young politicians solved weighty problems and planned conspiracies over gently rotated brandy snifters at the Cafe Nacional, just across from the lovely Parque Bolivar. There, lovers flirted at a distance while vendors sold flowers and trinkets to casual shoppers.

It was a remarkable era. A surface atmosphere of genteel customs hid a welling sub-current of steaming furies of personal and political rivalry. One July, as the strains of music floated across the streets, a Col. Perdomo Herera and Arturo Gomez left the Cafe Nacional and shot each other before surprised crowds on what is today the Cuarta Calle Oriental, near the Omnisport. Gentlemen shook their heads at the lack of social grace demonstrated by these two men, twiddled finely varnished walking canes topped with monogrammed solid gold handles, adjusted their carnation boutonnieres, rearranged the folded, starched points of carefully placed handkerchiefs, checked their heavy gold watches firmly secured at the end of a gold chain, and continued down the street to a rendezvous at the Salon Rosado.

Platters of turtle eggs and chicken in beer, and a one-peso half bottle of *vino* were served by harried waiters in white jackets. Robbery and street crime were rare. The night was filled with the sweet perfume of orange blossoms and mournful tunes of a marimba from lovers' serenades played under discreetly opened windows.

Orchestras played in the kiosk of the Parque Dueños, as small, charming mule-powered trolley cars noisily clattered down the narrow rails. Shade trees protected the curious as they rested on steel and wood benches and snacked on sweet *melcochas* and crunchy pork rinds. On the Calle del Calvaris and Sexta Avenida, an occasional heavy rainstorm would turn the sewerless street into a river, sidewalk to sidewalk. Portable bridges — heavy wooden planks on wheels — were then used to ferry people across the flooded streets. The damage done by the terrible earthquake of June 7, 1927 had given parts of San Salvador new and interesting buildings. But the charm of narrow, dark cobblestone streets, wood and wrought iron balconies, eclectic turrets and roof lines, multi-colored doors and shutters, remained for decades.

This was El Salvador at the turn of the century. But to fully understand that land, we must look further into the past.

El Salvador's history is an amalgamation of pre-Columbian Indians and Spanish and European immigrants joined marble-cake fashion into a small but distinct nation.

Pre-Columbian El Salvador was a sparsely populated region with an indigenous Indian population, the Pipil, who had developed a stable, relatively advanced culture. Through constant migration, alliances, and wars, the Pipil maintained close relationships with neighboring societies in what is today Guatemala and Honduras. In 1534, Pedro de Alvarado, one of Hernan Cortez's principal aides in the conquest of Mexico, set out to conquer what is now Guatemala and El Salvador. He crossed the Paz River into El Salvador in June at Cuscatlán near today's San Salvador. The Spaniards marched into battle, only to be soundly defeated by the Pipil Indians. It was one of the few serious setbacks to the Spanish in their conquest of the New World. Alvarado, wounded in the campaign, retreated to Guatemala. After recovering from his wounds, he prepared a new assault against the Pipil Indians.

The counter-offensive was strong and violent, and in 1525, Alvarado finally subjugated the Pipil. Miller, Baily, and Nasatir write: "The whole story of the (Spanish) conquest of Nicaragua, Costa Rica, El Salvador, and Panama is one of cruelty . . . The Indians were the ones to suffer most, being subject to every outrage, and were murdered and enslaved by the thousands. . . "

The conquerors of Central America were the same genre as those who exterminated the Caribes on the Island of Hispanola. They overran the Aztecs in central Mexico, and enslaved hundreds of thousands in the silver and gold mines of Potosi. These men, motivated by gold and glory, rode roughshod over complex societies; by our standards, the conquistadors violated every principle of civilized society. Yet they were men who carried out their conquest in the name of the Lord, converting with cross and sword men, women and children to the "true faith" — Roman Catholicism. The outrages committed in the pursuit of greed and religion were finally brought to the attention of the Spanish crown by Friar Bartolome de la Casas. His work, *Brevissima Relacion*, was translated into English and published in London in 1656. He wrote of the Spaniards:

> . . . Their cruelty did not take pity even on women
> with children, whose bellies they ripped up, taking
> out the infants to hew them to pieces. They would
> often lay wagers as to who could cleave or cut a man
> through the middle with the most dexterity, or who
> could cut off his head at one blow. The children they
> would take by the feet and dash their innocent heads
> against rocks, and when they were fallen in the water,
> the Spaniards would call upon them to swim with a
> strange and cruel derision. Sometimes they would
> run both the mother and unborn infant through in
> one thrust.

Thus did the proud Pipil Indians and the arrogant Spaniards come together in violence. Once the Salvadoran Indians were conquered, the Spanish settled in the region and intermarried with the natives. The absence of mineral wealth left the colony in the backwater of Spanish rule for the next 250 years. Its population grew slowly. By the end of the 18th century, farms prospered and indigo — the principal crop — brought wealth to this new land. At the beginning of the 19th century, San Salvador was the largest city of the Capitancy of Guatemala. Interestingly, El Salvador was the first of the five components of the Spanish colony to strike a blow for independence from Spain. A priest, Jose Matias Delgado, led an uprising in 1811, which was put down, but served to spark uprisings in other parts of Central America.

Independence from Spanish rule came on September 15, 1821, some seven months after Augustin de Iturbide success-fully led the movement against colonial rule in Mexico. Iturbide declared himself emperor and invited the Central American provinces to join his empire. Only El Salvador refused, insist-ing on Central American autonomy. When Iturbide's expe-ditionary force attempted to forcefully conquer the rebels, El Salvador strongly resisted and petitioned the United States for statehood. The U.S. Congress did not act, and the matter ended when Iturbide was overthrown. The United Provinces of Central America was established in 1823 as a federation. It was not a truly "united" federation, as the comments of John Stephens, on an 1839 mission to represent President Van Buren suggests. Looking for the federal authorities in Guatemala, Stephens mused, ". . . it was incumbent upon me to look around for the government to which I was accredited."

Two historians have described Mr. Stephens' dilemma thus: "Where was the national capital? Was it Guatemala City. . . ? No. Guatemala City was in the control of a twenty-three year old Indian named Rafael Carrera, a despot supported only by the Guatemalan conservatives and abjured by other regions. Was the capital Quetzaltenango, Guatemala's second city which had just declared itself a separate province in the federation? No. Just before Stephens' arrival, a mob of frenzied women had stoned to death the federal vice-president who had come to collect federal taxes there. The federal military commander maintained his headquarters in San Salvador, but only the people of that city themselves considered it the federal capital."

This Central American fragmentation characterized not only politics, it involved religious groups as well. A church group had become angered that El Salvador was not to be a separate diocese. Its members started a revolt against the federal government, precipitating a civil war in which a young Honduran, Francisco Morazan, led the combined Salvadoran and Honduran forces to victory, temporarily ruling over a "pacified" federation in 1830. Morazan was a liberal who triggered fear and hatred among the conservative elites. They backed an Indian pig farmer, Rafael Carrera (the despot Stephens found in Guatemala), who they felt would reclaim the provinces from the threatening Morazan. Carrera organized Indian armies against Morazan in part by telling the poor that he, (Carrera) was the Archangel Rafael. Carrera captured Guatemala City, was driven out by an army which Morazan led from El Salvador, only to retake the city and Guatemala a year later.

Historian Hubert Herring says that "The Indians regarded Carrera as their messiah, hailed him as *Hijo de Dios* "Son of God", and *Nuestro Señor*, "Our Lord." He was decorated by the Pope for his services to the faith and by President Santa Anna of Mexico for his fidelity to conservatism. The creole landowners, foreigners, and the clergy, while privately deploring his ignorance, supported Carrera because of his firm stand for religion and property rights and his almost absolute control over the masses. He maintained peace and security within his nation, improved roads, encouraged efficient farming, handled public money honestly, and reduced the national debt. But he was despotic and ruthless with all who opposed his

will. Under him Guatemalans learned nothing of self government. He was responsible for continued turmoil in El Salvador,
Honduras, and Nicaragua, intervening again and again to place
fellow conservatives in power. Carrera's slogan was, "Long
live religion — death to foreigners." Stephens was the first
and, it is said, perhaps the last foreigner to meet Carrera.

Carrera maintained power in Guatemala and, indirectly in
neighboring El Salvador, for a quarter of a century, until his
death in 1863. Often the target of assassination attempts and
twice temporarily exiled, he held on to his office in part by
re-writing the constitution so that only the upper classes could
hold citizenship. Carrera's impact on El Salvador was important.
Among other things, he installed Francisco Malespin, commander of the Salvadoran army, as president in 1840. Later,
in 1843, Malespin was to become the first elected chief executive of that country.

Like most Latin American countries, El Salvador's 19th
century political history was marked by bloody confusion
and political instability. One historian noted that between
1843 and 1900, there were twelve revolutions, five coup d'etats
and two presidents executed by firing squad.

Some of the changes of power in El Salvador were both
curious and amusing. General Carlos Erzeta, for example,
was appointed army commander by President Francisco
Menendez and given a mandate to crush one of many incipient
revolutions. The clever general was invited to a ball given in
President Menendez's honor. Once at the ball, he took the
opportunity to seize the president, execute him, and take
over the presidency. Guatemala, which had backed the hapless
dead former chief executive, refused to recognize General
Erzeta and declared war on El Salvador. In the struggle, the
general himself was ousted from office.

Central America is plagued with mountains and forests
more difficult to cross than the waters separating the Caribbean
Islands. It is a region of small towns, distant and infrequently

traveled. However, El Salvador was considered to be more progressive and productive than its neighbors. Dictators and palace revolts should have had no place in a land with such great agricultural potential.

Yet inter-party strife between liberals and conservatives, backed by powerful armies, periodic revolutions, and constant border conflicts with Guatemala and Nicaragua kept El Salvador under autocratic rule. Still, on the whole, its policies compared favorably with those of its other Central American neighbors. El Salvador actually experienced fewer assassinations and even less political violence. Nonetheless, according to Victor Alba, El Salvador underwent no less than 117 military coups in roughly 138 years.

One of the most significant developments in El Salvador during the late nineteenth century was the speed with which the so-called "Period of Anarchy" was modified through liberal reform. The colonial economic underpinnings, based on indigo and subsistence farming communities, disappeared in less than forty years. This was a much shorter period than in any of the neighboring countries. Communal and Indian lands, covering forty to fifty per cent of the territory, quickly became private property, most of it controlled by coffee growers and wealthy landowners. This liberalism in economic affairs formed the seeds of the current economic structure. As a result of the transformation of agriculture, mercantile and capitalist systems of production came into being. Employment and livelihood patterns changed. The country was flooded very quickly with a so-called proletarian or semi-proletarian rural labor force which sold its labor for wages. Salvadoran historians point out that this provided a growing army of job seekers. It also contributed to an accelerated population explosion and its attendant emigration to Honduras. Both issues came into full bloom eighty years later. What is significant about these rather violent economic shifts is the rapid consolidation of a powerful capitalist oligarchy on the one hand and an immense labor force on the other. The Marxist concept of class struggle, pitting capitalists against the proletarian, thus occured in an unlikely area. However these consequences of economic liberalism were not yet evident on the surface of Salvadoran society.

Politically, toward the end of the nineteenth century, El Salvador faced problems from the pull and push from its neighbors (Honduras, Nicaragua, and Guatemala) whose political leaders and dictators still retained hope of a unified Central America. In 1903 Nicaraguan dictator José Santos Zelaya directly intervened in Honduras' internal political succession problems. Then he turned his attention to El Salvador, targeted as the next country in his scheme for Central American unification. Zelaya's backing of Salvadoran rebels led Salvadoran President Pedro Jose Escalon to turn to the United States for help. Through the general intervention and mediation of President Theodore Roosevelt and Secretary of State Elihu Root, Zelaya was dissuaded from pursuing his political objectives in El Salvador. Protected by international guarantees, the small coffee-planter oligarchy of El Salvador was able to reach agreement to transfer power peacefully. The assassination of Manuel E. Araujo in 1913 by gunmen, as he sat under a tree, was considered to be the result of a personal grudge. So peaceful was the situation, that the presidency was held between 1913 and 1927 by members of one family, the Melendez family.

No candidate received a majority in the relatively free election of 1931. The man chosen by the legislature as president was unpopular; an uprising in December 1931, together with the withdrawal of support by the military, led to his downfall. His constitutional successor, vice-president, General Maximiliano Hernandez Martinez, became president in 1932. Martinez assumed power during the shock of a world-wide depression which pushed down coffee prices, causing great poverty and unrest throughout Latin America. The depression precipitated a wave of new governments. These were a different breed of regime, mostly led by military officers who seized on the unrest and violence which accompanied the Great Depression. The period from 1930 to 1939 served as a turning point in Latin American politics. By and large, it ended the struggles between liberal and conservative parties and set aside issues such as strongly centralized vs. decentralized government and secularization vs. continued close linkage between the church and state, especially in education. Yet it seriously curtailed any growing movement toward greater social change.

Salvadoran President General Martinez came to power at a time when even democratic countries like Chile and Uruguay could not overcome the wave of crises, succumbing to military rule or military-backed leadership.

The Colombian writer Germán Arciniegas called Martinez a wizard. Martinez was a Theosophist. Theosophy is a mystical religion based upon a mixture of Eastern and Western teachings. Martinez's Theosophist mysticism manifested itself in a curious set of beliefs and behavior patterns. He thought, for example, that bottles filled with colored water and placed on the roof of the presidential palace — after brewing in the sun — would cure cancer, rheumatism, heart disease and all manner of ailments. He also believed that since animals did not wear shoes children should not wear them either, so that they might "receive the vibrations of the earth."

Arciniegas wrote that Martinez once said, "It is a greater crime to kill an ant than a man, for when a man dies he becomes reincarnated, while the ants die forever." For this reason Martinez never killed ants. His views on people, on the other hand, were somewhat different. When a force of impoverished peons formed a communist Red Army in the vicinity of the town of Izalco, killing plantation owners, Martinez quickly responded, capturing and executing an estimated 10,000.

While Arciniegas believed that this figure was probably an exaggeration, it does suggest something of the mind processes of the then president of El Salvador.

For the communists, of course, this event was not only a disaster but a rallying point for future struggle. The communist uprising in El Salvador in the early 1930s resulted, according to leftist figures, in the death of up to 30,000 peasants and Marxists. Even then one communist writer commented, perhaps a bit optimistically, that "At the present time, it [the Salvadoran Communist Party] is being rebuilt."

Among those killed during this period was a young Trotskyite, Agustin Farabundo Marti, the son of Indian peasants. His name, unlike many of his unfortunate contemporaries, has not been lost to history. Marti is remembered as one of the founders of the Salvadoran Communist Party in March 1930, and he was one of the handful of Salvadorans who fought with the leftist revolutionary hero Sandino in Nicaragua. In 1932, he perished in the uprising so brutally crushed by President Martinez. But today one of the most active and visible Salvadoran guerrilla forces is named after Marti.

After crushing the communist rebellion in El Salvador, President Martinez consolidated his power, and tightened his control over the reigns of government throughout the 1930s and early 1940s. He manipulated El Salvador's election laws and forced the legislature to extend his tenure another five years, to 1950. But that act was apparently too much for many of the students, soldiers and voters. Sensing a threat to order, the leading families backed the military in yet another coup d'etat, but this time with a difference. Once in control, the military did not then turn the reign of government over to civilian authority. This 1944 coup marked the emergence of the military as perhaps the most dominant force in Salvadoran internal politics.

One cannot help but draw parallels between the political evolution of El Salvador from pre-Columbian times until 1945 and current events. Several themes offer threads of continuity. First of all, violence and cruelty mark the very beginning of Spanish-Pipil interaction. This was an unusually fierce relationship in which Spain suffered one of its very few defeats. Second, from its very inception, the church made up an important part of the political life of the country. The Spanish conquistadors suppressed the local population in the name of the Lord, and in 1811, Father Delgado was the first to call for a national revolt against Spain. Third, El Salvador's history has always been strongly affected by the actions of its neighbors. From Emperor Iturbide's try to incorporate El Salvador into his empire, to the constant machinations of Guatemalan, Honduran, and Nicaraguan leaders, the country has had to fight for its very existence. Fourth, on several occasions — notably in 1823 when it asked to be incorporated into the United States and again in 1903 when it sought U.S. protection against Nicaragua's Zelaya — El Salvador has looked toward the United States as an external force which could help balance out unfavorable regional pressures. Fifth, and finally, El Salvador has had a difficult if interesting domestic political evolution. Many of its leaders brought about structural and technical changes such as road building, sanitation, eradication of epidemic diseases, new housing, and the construction of ports and rail lines. However, political development has always lagged behind. Colorful and sometimes even popular figures assumed the presidency. Yet political participation and the right to question fundamental social and economic conditions never was legitimized. In El Salvador only modest differences of political opinion were considered acceptable. El Salvador is one of very few nations in this hemisphere which experienced a major upheaval in the early 1930s, inspired by a local communist uprising. This event has played a powerful historical, symbolic, and political role in every subsequent political event in that nation.

As we analyze the transitional period from the old system

to the current crisis, this political archeology must be kept
in mind. It is a crucial set of prejudices, experiences, ideological and cultural assumptions out of which every living
Salvadoran grew. It is the social memory, the oral and written
history, the family and regional legacy — in a word the political culture — of modern Salvador. Without it, one cannot
fully comprehend the events taking place in the 1980s.

4

The Armed Forces
Become Political

El Salvador ". . . is the only country in Latin America in which the armed forces organization is both leading and supporting the nation along the pathway of democratic, evolutionary, and social revolution," wrote Edwin Liewen in 1964. This optimistic and positive assessment came at a time when El Salvador seemed to be at the peak of an army-led experiment in socio-economic reform. This transition sought to reconcile the cleavages and violence caused by the long and divisive Martinez administration and its predecessors. Following his overthrow, the armed forces under General Castañeda Castro maintained order through martial law and strong repressive

45

measures which ended in the "Revolution of 1948." Disgusted with the harshness of the past four years, radical-leaning colonels and majors, backed by reformist civilians, removed the incumbent government and set up a five-man military-civilian junta. The *New York Times* reported on December 16, 1948, that the junta promised honest government, sweeping reforms, and respect for the constitution.

Hubert Herring, in his *A History of Latin America,* observed that,"El Salvador's armed forces have been mavericks. The increasing concern of the army. . . for the economic and social well-being of the country reflects some stirring of conscience among able and honest military leaders."

It was obvious to the more intelligent and educated military leaders that the Marxist alternative was increasingly being offered to the masses as a viable alternative to years of neglect.

It is difficult to reconstruct how Latin American political leaders perceived the threat of communism in the post World War I period, because we tend to identify a global Marxist offensive with the Cold War which came after the Second World War. Nonetheless, it appears that the symbols and images of Latin anti-communism were forged in the 1920s and 1930s. Not only did El Salvador in the 1932 peasant revolt experience domestic mobilization, activism, and revolutionary activity by Marxist-Leninist and Trotskyite groups, but indeed that force had swept through Latin America. When Martinez crushed the uprising in Izalco, he was only one of at least eight Latin American leaders to do so. Indeed, communist subversion appears to have been a hemisphere-wide problem. The 1948 Revolution in El Salvador should be seen in front of this backdrop of genuine concern with outside agitation, the erosion of power in the old regimes, unrest, and a real criticism of existing social conditions.

A constitution ratified in 1950 provided new and more liberal ground rules: it extended suffrage to both males and females eighteen years and older; it recognized the state's obligation to expand health, education, and social services; it ruled that the armed forces were to be nonpolitical and obedient to the government in power; it limited the president to one six-year term in office; and it made the judiciary an independent body. Reformist factions in the military began to sense an activist role for themselves precisely at a time when the constitution prohibited the armed forces from engaging in politics. Minister of Interior, and later president, Colonel Jose Maria Lemus, expressed the spirit of the new armed forces in an address marking the third anniversary of the 1948 Revolution:

> In order to conduct the 1948 Revolution, the army had to withdraw itself from the influence of the existing political climate and identify itself with the popular will, in order to form for itself an adequate mentality, with the end of responding to the imperatives of the democratic world movement. . . The army exists. . . not to enthrone tyrannies. . . (but) to observe the sacred institutional postulates of fulfilling the law and of being the guardian of the national sovereignty. . . The army is not a static institution. . . In effect the army is the force which represents the right of the people. . . It is an institution with a conscience. . . The army is the main bulwark in defense of the popular rights which were so valiantly fought for in the 1948 Revolution.

This statement is a model of Latin American armed forces self-perception. A new political party, the Partido Revolucionario de Unificación Democratica (PRUD) was founded. A weaker opposition party, the Partido Acción Renovadora

(PAR) backed a rival candidate.

PRUD was to become a dominant force for over a decade. Despite protestations that the military was non-political, its leaders, including Major Oscar Osorio and Colonel Lemus himself, ran for and won the presidency in 1950 and again in 1956. Civilians such as Roberto Canessa, who in 1956 sought the presidency, backed by the Partido Acción Nacional (PAN), found themselves at a disadvantage. Canessa was disqualified on a technicality from running a month before the election.

PRUD in the late 1950s sought to expand social welfare and infrastructural programs within the government without threatening the social order. Success at local elections in 1958 and 1960 did not, however, mask the growing activity of new political groups which sought to fundamentally challenge the traditional legacies of poverty and underdevelopment. Colonel Lemus began to rule as a moderate. He declared a general amnesty for political prisoners and invited exiles back. He voided laws which were repressive and appointed to the administration people who were recognized for their sober and technical approach to national problems.

Whatever his intentions, Colonel Lemus's policies were soon undermined by a steady decline in coffee and cotton prices. Falling prices seriously damaged the fragile economy and affected the social fabric of the country. Political unrest began to grow. There were efforts at Central American integration, including the establishment of a Salvadoran Development Institute, which was to play a vital role in carrying out the nation's five-year plan. Bureaucrats were trained under contract with the Public Administration Service of Chicago and a host of other ambitious projects were begun, including highway construction financed by the Inter-American Bank; a laboratory built by the Armour Research Foundation to stimulate new industry; a cement factory and textile plant financed by Japanese capital; and the construction of the Rio Lempa Dam, which doubled the country's electrical output, allowing for the irrigation of 85,000 acres of previously fallow land. In addition, all five Central American nations helped finance a Sherwin Williams paint factory, the United Nations assisted in the expansion of port facilities at Acajutla, and a private company undertook the construction of a major sugar refinery.

A correspondent for *The Christian Science Monitor* toured El Salvador in April 1953, and reported that "the people are eager to learn new methods, according to technicians. This explains the presence of more foreign specialists per square mile than perhaps in any other country in the world." American foreign aid, experts from the World Health Organization, a Rockefeller Foundation group as well as the United Nations Children's Fund were listed by the correspondent as among the key experts seeking to solve the so-called "age old problems" of poverty, illiteracy, poor housing and bad water in El Salvador.

All these efforts proved insufficient, however. In 1959 Fidel Castro overthrew Fulgencio Batista in Cuba, opening a new era in hemispheric politics. In El Salvador, the world coffee recession led to conspiracies by powerful economic groups, afraid that the modest socio-economic reforms would undermine their wealth and power. Both the left, which was now inspired by the idea of instant Cuban-model revolution, and the right, which yearned for an opportunity to reverse the modest reforms of the past ten years, pressured the government. The April 24, 1960 elections proved to be a major turning point in Salvadoran political history.

Reformist groups organized the National Front of Civic Orientation, seeking seats in congress and in local assemblies. Colonel Lemus, harassed and apprehensive, claimed the National Front had been infiltrated by communists. Rules regulating political parties were changed, making it very difficult for the opposition to put up candidates. The new law also banned parties with communist or anarchist members from running for office.

In August 1960, the Foreign Ministers of the American States met in San Jose, Costa Rica. The agenda dealt mainly with Cuba and the need for sanctions against the new Castro regime. In El Salvador opposition groups — some claim they were mostly communists — took the opportunity to launch massive demonstrations which turned into riots. The army moved in, violently crushing the riots. Students went on strike on August 25. A state of siege was imposed by the legislature on September 5. President Lemus announced that he had discovered a communist plot to overthrow the government of El Salvador. Riots and violence escalated, resulting in a number of deaths. Finally, on October 26, 1960, the army deposed Lemus.

A junta composed of three army officers and three civilians set about to reorganize the government, releasing all political prisoners, purging the bureaucracy, and announcing wide-ranging reforms. However, mass demonstrations escalated, and the streets of San Salvador were in the hands of what at the time were called *Fidelistas*, sympathizers of the Cuban leader, Fidel Castro, and communists. At the same time in late 1960 two new parties were formed: a Social Democratic Party backed by former President Osorio, and a leftist party called the Revolutionary Party of April and May.

El Salvador in 1960 and early 1961 presents a tangled political montage. Leftist agitation increased while General Osorio made a new bid for power. He was opposed by many of the conservative elite who identified Osorio with the major reforms of the past decade. From this confusion stemmed the coup d'etat of January 25, 1961. A new civilian-military directorate assumed power, forcing General Osorio into exile. It promised a strong anti-communist program. A junta-sponsored National Conciliation Party (PCN) was founded. Naturally the new government was opposed by both the extreme left and the extreme right — a pattern which is the trademark of Salvadoran politics. Notwithstanding, the new junta pushed through

335 different laws aimed at reforming the social and economic problems which it saw as causing El Salvadoran instability. The civil service was reformed, the leading bank nationalized, and foreign exchange controls were enacted, designed to reduce flight of capital. The junta established a social security system, reduced rents by thirty per cent, increased the minimum wage and established rent ceilings. The new government aided the poor of El Salvador, but the rich and elite factions in that country were not impressed.

The leader of this new junta was Lt. Colonel Julio Adalberto Rivera, a generally popular figure not identified with either the left or the right. He was regarded as a competent administrator. Colonel Rivera's progressive and reformist program hurt the rich of El Salvador most, particularly the new income tax, which ran at a rate of over 76 per cent for incomes in excess of $78,000 U.S. dollars. It was not surprising when some of the most powerful families in the land accused the junta — and particularly Colonel Rivera — of being communists. Rivera resigned from the junta, and power was assumed by an interim civilian government. Colonel Rivera decided to run for the presidency and was supported in this endeavor by the National Conciliation Party. Opposition groups boycotted the election, claiming it would be fraudulently conducted. This is a pattern typical of El Salvador as well as other Latin American nations. Authorities generally agree that the popular Colonel Rivera would most probably have won against any candidate. However the refusal of opposition parties to field candidates deprived the new government of complete legitimacy.

The Rivera Government from 1962 to 1967 was generally considered to have ushered in a period of unprecedented peace, constitutional restraint, honesty, and competent leadership. Some of the major reforms instituted by the Rivera Government were a land reform program which distributed plots of land to 3,500 poor families, the enactment of new minimum wage laws which included pay but no work for

Sundays, food allowances for farm workers, another new income tax law and a series of credit programs designed to assist small farmers. Under Rivera, the El Salvadoran economy began to grow again, and the nation's per capita gross national product made sizable gains.

Colonel Fidel Sanchez Hernandez was elected president in 1967. Sanchez moved into the presidency committed to continue the reform initiated by his predecessor. However, he inherited a nation plagued by land shortage, excessive population, and virtually no national resources (such as minerals) which could become the basis for a major and costly national transformation. El Salvador was a poor, overcrowded country. In fact, President Rivera had initiated contacts with neighboring states to attempt a historic, unprecedented solution to overpopulation. He suggested to land-rich and sparsely-populated Nicaragua that Salvadoran farmers be allowed to migrate and settle there to develop new lands. He began negotiations with Honduras in an attempt to normalize and legalize the status of illegal Salvadoran emigrants living and farming in that neighboring nation. It was estimated by the late 1960s that over 300,000 illegal Salvadorans were living in Honduras. This serious problem was to erupt into perhaps the major crisis of contemporary Salvadoran history — the 1969 war with Honduras.

Salvadoran-Honduran relations deteriorated and reached a critical point after Honduran land reform programs began to adversely affect Salvadorans living there. In July 1969, riots broke out at an emotional soccer game between the two countries. Honduran mobs attacked Salvadorans, ending the game with bloodshed. The Salvadoran press reported atrocities by Hondurans against hapless Salvadoran peasants. Border tensions increased, skirmishes occurred, and both sides converted old transport airplanes for military use. El Salvador attacked Santa Rosa de Copan and Toncontin Airport in

Tegucigalpa. Honduras retaliated by attacking El Salvador's Ilopango Airport and Acajutla. The military forces of both countries were meagerly supplied and equipped, mostly by the United States. Antiquated weapons, practically no aircraft, and short combat supply inventory did not stop the armed forces of both countries from engaging in fierce combat.

> President Sanchez put on his. . . uniform and led troops into the field. A three pronged attack yielded quick results and allowed the Salvadoran army to penetrate twenty-five miles into Honduras. The 12,000 residents of Ocotepeque fled in panic.

The "soccer war" presented the Salvadoran government with a series of major burdens and responsibilities. For a poor nation the expenditure of a substantial part of its military supplies and resources is, indeed, a luxury. This is especially true because the suspicion, tension, and war-jitters continued long after the Organization of American States managed to arrange a truce after just two weeks of fighting. Re-supplying the military became a matter of vital national self interest. Casualties, including 3,000 to 4,000 dead on both sides and thousands of wounded, were also a burdensome tragedy which consumed several years' worth of normal expenditures in public health services and medicine.

The Central American economies by the end of the decade of the 1960s had become quite interdependent. Between 1961 and 1969, the Central American Common Market (CACM) had brought about the elimination of most tariff barriers between the member countries. This yielded an increase of over seven hundred per cent in interregional trade, stimulating a boom in small business and industry, a mild incentive for agricultural production, and the flow of persons across borders for trade and tourism. By 1968, the area's more developed countries — Guatemala and El Salvador — were clearly dominating intraregional trade, and had benefited most from CACM. The "soccer war" seriously disrupted this integration process.

The impact of a trade dispute on El Salvador and Honduras cannot be overestimated. A sudden loss of its major marketing routes — overland roads — and one of its more important trade partners, Honduras, created unemployment, stagnation in the investment for new industry, conservative behavior by capital as well as a slump in the housing and construction industry. Moreover, the war had disrupted the overall process of co-operation and integration of the Central American states, a process which had been pursued by the Organization of Central American States (ODECA) founded in 1951. ODECA's headquarters was in San Salvador, and the organization's main legal instrument is the "Charter of San Salvador."

Finally, the 1969 war created a massive flood of Salvadoran refugees who poured back into their homeland in the face of great hostility and repeated brutalities at the hands of the Hondurans. One Salvadoran administrator estimated the return flow in the hundreds of thousands. It may have amounted to somewhere between five and eight per cent of the total population of El Salvador. This is truly a staggering challenge to any society, especially one which is structurally underdeveloped and simply incapable of coping with such a surge of dependent citizens coming on top of the other disruption of war. One can imagine the impact of close to twenty million unemployed, sick, and completely destitute people flooding the United States in a matter of a few weeks.

Even before the war, Salvadorans were living a hand-to-mouth existence. Herring writes: "It was estimated in 1961 that less than 0.1 per cent of the landholders owned some 16 per cent of the farmland, in haciendas of 2,472 acres or more; while at the other extreme about 85 per cent of the farmers, holding less than 15 per cent of the farmland, were hard put to make a living from their meager plots of 12.4 acres or less." An average day's wage was a mere 50 cents.

Colonel Sanchez had inherited a country which was moving, albeit slowly, toward reforms intended to change precisely these conditions. He was struggling against the legacy of four generations of wealthy Salvadoran oligarchs. His best efforts to continue the socio-economic and political reforms initiated by his predecessor President Rivera is clear from reading assessments made at the time. One analyst suggested that ". . . the improvements in housing, education, public health, and transportation are all signs that the traditional ruling aristocracy no longer controls the country and that a viable political system is emerging." Another writer, Peter Calver, called El Salvador's politicians ". . . left wing leadership," and wrote about the Central American Common Market's impact on El Salvador as having not only helped constitutional government but as also having accelerated democratic progress.

Politically the Sanchez government was also on stronger ground than most previous regimes. Sanchez was elected president in the first election in El Salvador where several candidates campaigned for office and in which it is generally assumed that election laws were conducted fairly. Sanchez won overwhelmingly with 223,746 votes primarily because of support and confidence in the policies of his predecessor and his identification with the National Conciliation Party. His opponents, however, were given the opportunity to begin building both political parties and a base of support for the future. Abraham Gonzalez, candidate of the Christian Democratic Party, received 90,089 votes. Fabio Castillo (Renovating Action) obtained 59,537, and Alvaro Martinez of the Popular Salvadoran Party received 38,647. The intentions and methods of the Conciliation party were, of course, moderate rather than radical or revolutionary, as its slogan "Evolution in Liberty" implies.

An evaluation in 1969, just prior to the outbreak of the "soccer war" said that, "Today El Salvador is closer to having a stable, functioning constitutional system than ever before in its history." That survey concluded that:

> All things considered, El Salvador seems to be on the brink of establishing democratic government. The introduction of proportional representation in the National Assembly has tended to strengthen the political parties and to make opposition to the government respectable, so there seems reason to hope that El Salvador will abandon the coup d'etat, revolution, and violence as political techniques in favor of democratic processes that will transform it into a progressive state of literate, prosperous people.

The "soccer war" and its aftermath proved a terrible reversal of this promising trend.

In El Salvador, as in the rest of Latin America, the threat of external revolutionary ideas coupled with Soviet support and instigation of communist uprisings led to a political realignment in the 1940s. Moreover, the world depression had proved a serious blow to *laissez-faire* economics, requiring more vigorous governmental intervention. In El Salvador the overthrow of the Martinez dictatorship and its replacement by an equally repressive regime led to a major polarization. For the first time, this rift also included the armed forces which split between reactionaries, conservatives, and reformers.

The 1948 Revolution marked the ascendency of progressive military leaders at least in the Salvadoran context of "Progressive." Presidents Osorio and Lemus were a departure from politics as usual. So also was the new constitution. Moderate reforms began to take hold. Changes in the 1950s were largely economic and led to a growth in governmental bureaucracy. The "developmental" policies of the two administrations in the 1950s were most strongly evident in attracting new investments and creating jobs. President Lemus, in particular, was well able to handle the rapidly growing economic opportunities and made the most of highway construction, land irrigation, and manpower training opportunities in the public sector. The fact that the rich, land speculators and bureaucrats also prospered from "development" was helpful. However, Colonel Lemus was not in a position to handle a new challenge coming from abroad.

In 1959 Fidel Castro marched into Havana, deposing Fulgencio Batista, setting in motion a new and revolutionary momentum which engulfed all of Latin America. In El Salvador, *fidelismo*, as it was then called, sent a cold shudder up the spines of conservative groups who had viewed the reforms of the last decade in their own country with some skepticism. Now they saw a potentially disastrous radicalism on the horizon which could totally remove them from economic and social power. Leftist revolutionary elements, on the other hand, saw in Castro's success a new hope and thus renewed their efforts.

The riots and violence of 1960 in San Salvador are classic examples of unrest in Latin America. Leftists and moderates surged through the streets. No one seemed in control. Communist agitators and terrorists infiltrated the demonstrations. Rightist secret police and agitators for ultra-conservative groups also made their way towards the central plaza. Suddenly shots rang out, rocks began to fly, people fell and trampled each other. Blood began to run; tear gas grenades exploded. People died. The result was an embarrassment to the government, and opened the potential for a coup d'etat. Indeed, that was the fate of Colonel Lemus in 1960. It is clear in the case of El

Salvador that both the extreme right and the left — especially the revolutionary Marxist groups — favored the destabilization of the government. Each hoped that its forces and supporters would then be able to seize the power — the right expecting to reverse some of the reforms of the past ten years, the left anxious to expand on the reforms, pushing towards total revolution.

As a preventive to either the reactionaries or the radicals, a civilian-military junta stepped in, but it too was unable to stem the pressures exerted by both the left and right. The second junta in January 1961 cracked down hard on unrest and violence but decided that "developmental reform" somewhere down the left of center of the political highway was the most realistic route. Indeed, the 1960s were the most encouraging period in Salvadoran history. Salvadorans seemed to have found a path of reform which could permit a modicum of political participation and a potential full blossoming of competitive democratic processes — the best one could expect given the conditions of poverty, overpopulation, and the political history as well as political culture and traditions of El Salvador. But the war with Honduras was to shatter all hope that the system could evolve.

As the country lurched forward toward the 1972 elections, hard times were indeed at hand. The 1970s were to be a tragic period of political retrenchment, reversal, and institutional erosion. The economic growth of the fifties and sixties slowed, and the bloom was soon to come off the flower of political diversification and tolerance.

5

The Rules of the Political Game

Grandchildren dashed in and out of the living room where channel 8 on the television flashed a message stressing the "need for more family communications." But Don Torinos' family was not listening. Mr. Torinos concentrated on his half-smoked Marlboro, sipping from his glass of pineapple juice and vodka. He grasped the glass with his worn, gnarled fingers, his hand shaking as he put it to his mouth.

Don Torinos was oblivious to all else. He slumped in his plastic covered chair, recalling the nightmare of his past years as a small-town mayor of the Christian Democratic Party.

"I never understood the polemics," he sighed, his frail

body slumping farther into the chair. His main concern had been putting electrical wiring into two schools, meeting the municipal payroll, remaining at peace with the central government, and assisting the poor by making improvements to the small local health center.

Torinos reminisced about the many nights that he walked to the police station to settle disputes or to look at a corpse brought in after a particularly violent drunken brawl. He often settled disputes between laborers and landowners by "just talking and pleading." The army, on the other hand, employed arrogance and brutality even in private disputes.

Torinos' eyes were filled with anxiety. "The extremist reactionaries considered a Christian Democrat, and especially a mayor, a communist. The word communist lingered on Torinos' tongue like a strange substance with a disagreeable taste. "Me, a communist! What stupidity! "

Torinos said that people like him were looked upon as "enemies of the people" by the extreme right as well as the extreme left. The leftists charged him with supporting the system that had contributed to the exploitation of workers and peasants. "The left claims I'm an ally of international imperialism and multinationals. Actually, I was just a poor mayor of a poor town in a poor country. No more. No less. I always tried to squeeze every cent out of the system for the poorest people in my town."

The anxiety created by being mayor made the sixty-year-old Torinos look like a tired man of eighty. "Any night I expect someone to walk through that door and pump lead into me," he said disinterestedly. "I don't know what will become of politics here because it doesn't work the way we've always said it should — with moderation, with recognition of the limits of what can be done, with peaceful change through election, and with respect for one another."

My conversation with Mr. Torinos ended. The grandchildren were asleep, the vodka was gone and the television station had signed off. The signature on the screen was like Salvadoran politics: clear one moment, jumbled another and then totally blank the next. Don Torinos took one last puff of his Marlboro and we said goodnight.

Thousands of Salvadorans are like my friend Don Torinos, caught in the middle or forced to take a position on the fringes of political extremism. To people like Torinos and to foreigners, Salvadoran politics seems incomprehensible. They may sense but surely do not grasp the patterns that are basic to Latin American society which are seen in exaggeration in El Salvador.

Contemporary Salvadoran politics, like that of many Latin American countries, can best be understood if we look at some of the unique features of Latin American society. Douglas Chalmers listed four factors: Latin American socio-political structure, he suggested, is characterized by the relative absence of true class conflict as well as a dearth of free and autonomous interest groups. It also has an inter-mingling of social and political structures, so that one often cannot tell where one ends and the other begins. There are confrontations and fluid alliances of the elites, each cluster of which has different power capabilities. Finally, there is a predominance of "technician-centered decision making style."

Chalmers suggests that neither class conflict nor the growth of independent interest groups have broken the connection between the upper and lower classes of society. The absence of class conflict stems from the cultivation of patron-client relations that tie poor to rich, peasant to landowner, and customer to shopkeeper. The ties that bind these groups are often reciprocal. For example, the landowner provides seasonal work, medicine, or a loan in exchange for the peasant's labor, his loyalty and his willingness to work for meager wages.

A similar reciprocal relationship exists between social and political elements. Social goals are difficult to pursue without cultivating ties to political officials or to the bureaucracy.

Many times gifts and status must be given to government agents to get something done. The overlapping of the social and political is seen in Salvadoran economic policy. This policy represents special interests of business, of profits, of kickbacks, and of benefits.

Various groups vie for power, utilizing their own ways and means. For some it may be strikes, for others mobilization of peasants, for others urban demonstrations, or electoral power, support from members of the armed forces, moral power, control of the media or use of economic resources. In the past two years, the use of violence has become a leading "power capability." Once violence was used just to gain recognition. Today, extreme violence is used by groups who do not want to yield power.

Adding to this struggle for power is the tradition of the technocrat formulating government policy. The policies of this group are formulated with little regard for domestic, social, and political problems. Many times the bureaucratic plan runs counter to powerful left or right-wing extremist groups, which causes great unrest and even bloodshed.

Together, these four factors help to explain the turbulence in El Salvador today. The tie between these very different groups has been sustained by necessity, tradition and violence. Of these diverse factions, the landowners have always had great economic and political power because they are the main producer of foreign exchange and domestic employment. The landowners also fare well in elections because their workers vote as they do. The commercial, industrial class has taken its place among the elite as a vital source of jobs, a stimulant to the construction industry and a link to international capital and technology. The military has become a predominant political factor by controlling the power shifts amongst various groups.

Salvadoran technical decision-making increased in the 1960s and 1970s. The national land reform program was initiated by the *técnico* elite and was criticized by both the left and the right because it worked against the existing power structure. The land reform program had more advocates in Washington, D.C. than in San Salvador.

Besides these contenders for power, labor unions, white collar workers, the professional and middle classes, foreign businessmen and advisors have also bid for power.

By increasing the level of violence, the various contending factions in El Salvador have produced a highly fragmented and volatile atmosphere. The blatant use of violence is a marked change for El Salvador where pressure has appeared traditionally in a more subtle form.

Violence necessitates organization and mobilization. El Salvador appears polarized by right-wing military and upper class supporters on one side, and leftists backed by workers and peasants on the other.

By the 1970s El Salvador was no longer a country divided into left and right, nor a nation controlled by landowning families. The military had superseded these families as the single most powerful institution in that land. The core of the military was no longer composed of sons of the wealthy, but rather a class of "new elite." Moreover, established political parties were no longer the focus of public mobilization. Instead, dozens of small parties, splintered factions, and a wide-range of front organizations competed with established organizations for loyalty. The ideological range of groups with power bases had widened.

Keeping this in mind, it seems that the 1979 coup can best be viewed as the disintergration of a precarious balance that held Salvadorans together. This balance included several features that are crucial to understanding the ferocity and extent of recent violence.

The landowners, threatened by an increasingly difficult military, formed an ultra-conservative military force called ORDEN. That group was organized with the help of a conservative former head of the National Guard, General Jose

Alberto Medrano, and an intelligence officer, Colonel Roberto D'Aubuisson. There were so many benefits — both civilian and military — that ORDEN grew to a size estimated ten times that of the national armed forces. ORDEN served as a cushion against leftist insurgent attack, particularly in rural areas. ORDEN also helped counterbalance quasi-military leftist organizations of peasants, farmers and communist revolutionaries.

Another feature that increased violence was the rapid growth of rural development programs in the 1970s. Some of these were church-sponsored, others were funded by private voluntary organizations, and some by the Salvadoran government. Conservative groups were fearful of poor people organizing. Innocuous self-help efforts such as food cooperatives, of literacy circles, nutrition and child care centers, and especially peasant legal-assistance groups were viewed as constituting challenges to the existing social-political order. And leftists formed, joined or controlled these reform groups.

Peasant organizers, cooperative leaders and people associated with self-help groups became the targets of torture and execution in 1980. *Campesino* groups were semi-officially labeled armed guerrillas by the extreme right. The irony of this is that the government encouraged the organization of these groups to carry out reform, especially land reform, but at the same time feared the power assumed by them. The government's contradictory view and subsequent actions caused the collapse of the original military-civilian reform junta in January 1980. When seven leading Christian Democrats resigned from their party and the government, they gave this as their reason: "A program of 'reforms and repression' runs contrary to the fundamentals of Christian Democracy. Agrarian reform must encompass not only the taking of lands from the major estate owners, but above all, the economic and political participation of peasant organizations."

A former official of the land reform agency, ISTA, reported

to a U.S. Congressional sub-committee that the targets of deaths investigated by his agency were ". . . peasants who were beginning to think, those peasants who wanted to participate in the political process."

Organization has been seen as one of the major challenges to tradition and to order. This is clear in Nicaragua where leftist and revolutionary groups such as the Sandinistas do not tolerate "independent" organizations of an economic, social, or self-help nature.

El Salvador remains divided on governmental, social, and economic reform. There is particular division concerning land reform. While class interest and self-interest of the landowners color the debate, the fundamental conflict is over the "sanctity of property." Socialist and redistributive formulas compete with neo-classic and *laissez faire* theories of property rights. The non-socialist approaches were not as well articulated as other groups so the line between those favoring free enterprise and the communists became more definite. This was true despite U.S. support of current land reform policies as non-communist alternatives. Current Salvadoran land reform is patterned after Taiwanese, Japanese and Korean reforms. These countries have highly productive, capitalistic agriculture on small farms achieved through expropriation of estates.

Political forces engaging in fratricide and decapitation are another major factor causing violence in El Salvador today. Political fratricide involves intense power struggles from within for control of opposition groups or for decision making positions in the government. Political decapitation occurs when groups kill the leaders of their opposition, literally cutting off the head of the organization.

The tactics of right-wing and revolutionary groups are geared to "erase the center." Moderate leaders within the government and among opposition groups have been subjected to the most violence.

The violence in El Salvador perpetuates itself. As violence

became a more effective political tool its use increased. As its use increased, violence became more extreme and more frequently used. The extreme violence that has divided the country into armed enclaves and the routine incidents of terrorism may not be the new rules of the political game in El Salvador, but it certainly has helped bring groups to power. Anyone familiar with the politics of Lebanon might be tempted to say that violence is a new rule of political competition. More than one political party has emerged through the use of violence. Regimes such as Hitler's German National Socialists and the Soviet Union under Stalin made a cult of death and terror.

According to observations made by Professor Antonio de Machados, Spanish politics parallel the rules of politics in El Salvador. He states that the only political gambit that has functioned with any precision is the reactionary one. "Leftists have rarely estimated, in discharging the rifle fire of their futuristic rhetoric, the recoil of the rifle stock that is often more jarring than the explosion itself."

In El Salvador it is the rifle fire, rather than the rhetoric that has recoiled upon the left. The recoil of violence also jars innocent bystanders like Don Torinos, who is caught between the extremes of both the left and the right.

6

On the Eve of
the 1972 Election

In September 1970, Chileans chose the first legally-elected Marxist president in Latin America. Cheering throngs, honking horns, and wild celebrating to the chant "A-llen-de, A-llen-de" marked the extraordinary event. When Salvador Allende defeated his Christian Democratic opponent Radomiro Tomic and Conservative Jorge Alessandri, a wave of surprise and shock went through the middle class country clubs, cafes, and elegant homes in cool, shaded suburbs all over Latin America. San Salvador was no different. While progressives and socialists celebrated Allende's victory, others blamed the rise of Chilean communism on the Christian Democrats under President

Eduardo Frei.   Salvadoran conservatives, as Stephen Webre relates it, felt that the Christian Democrats ". . . had through the enactment of irresponsible social reforms undercut the foundations of Chilean society and, thus, prepared the way for the communist enslavement of the country."

It is February 11, 1971, in San Salvador's fashionable neighborhood of Colonia Escalón.   A light breeze rustles the bushes and trees.   A bus swerves to avoid a stray dog.   Ernesto Regaldo Dueñas, thirty-five, was last seen on the sidewalk walking down the street in this prosperous section of town.   When the ransom message came, it was a demand for one million dollars cash.   Regaldo's family on both the father and mother's side are powerful, wealthy industrialists.   They had no problem raising the money.   It was never collected.   Seven days later a phone call brought the terrible news.   Ernesto's body, two bullet holes through his head, was found lying along a ditch in San Antonio Abad, a suburb of the capital city.   Salvadorans were enraged.   Webre concludes that, "The Regaldo murder must have seemed, not only to oligarchs but also to Salvadorans of all classes who valued social order, like the first trumpet in a campaign of leftist slaughter."

The Regaldo's traced their family far back into the nation's history.   General Tomás Regaldo was the man who in 1898 pulled El Salvador out of the Greater Republic of Central America by overthrowing Salvadoran President Rafael Antonio Gutiérrez.   He led a pragmatic liberal government until 1903. Regaldo reinforced Salvadoran sovereignty in 1902 by insulting the Guatemalan delegate and ending another union effort. On his mother's side we find Francisco Dueñas, the last of the clericalist (Catholic-church oriented) conservatives of the nineteenth century, who came to power in 1851 as a moderate conservative.   He was reinstated in 1863 and overthrown in 1871 through the connivance of Guatemalan strong man, Justo Rufino Barrios. Another Dueñas, Ricardo Dueñas Van Severen, is the author of several important politico-historical studies including the *Biografia del General Francisco Morazan* (1961) and *La Invasion Filibustera de Nicaragua y la Guerra Nacional* (1959).

This attack against one of the old and distinguished families raised a number of questions. Why was he executed? Who killed him? The conclusion reached was that members of a small cadre of persons inside the National University called "El Grupo," which included young Marxists as well as members of the Christian Democratic Party youth organizations had been responsible. Regalado's kidnapping, it is assumed, was the first in a series of extortion kidnappings to raise funds for the organization's activities. Parallels were immediately drawn with other West Euorpean terrorist organizations.

Latin American universities, including those in El Salvador, have always been the center of political activity. In colonial times forbidden books, including Tom Paine and the French encyclopedists, were read there. Later, the intellectual debates between liberalism and conservatism found fertile soil in the university setting. The most significant event, however, occurred in 1918 when Gabriel del Mazo began the University Reform Movement at the University of Cordoba, Argentina. This soon spread and was instituted in almost all Latin American countries. The movement demanded that government stay out of higher education. It asked for greatly increased funding, open enrollment to democratize higher education, and "self government," giving the universities control of curriculum and naming professors. Co-government, in which students and administrators shared power, was implemented. It also established the inviolability of university campuses. The national police and the armed forces could not enter the universities quasi-sovereign territory.

While academic freedom was gained through this, the

campuses also became battlegrounds for political wars to control the student organizations and take over the curriculum and programs. Nationalists, Christian Democrats, liberals, communists, socialists, Peking-oriented Marxists, anarchists, Trotskyites, pro-Cuban socialists, and conservatives all struggled, often violently. Under harsh dictatorships the universities were often the only place where competitive political forces survived. They were more than once the refuge for threatened politicians who could not reach the safety of a foreign embassy.

By the late 1960s, it is argued, the context of university life and university politics had changed. Alba wrote in 1968 that ". . . today, students show the same enthusiasm in combating regimes that are more or less democratic with the purpose not of improving them but of destroying them. It is students who form the guerrilla bands . . . and who were dedicated to terrorism in Venezuela (even after civilian democratic rule became the norm)."

Alba analyzes the situation by suggesting that the leftist and revolutionary orientation of universities may largely be due to the sense of inadequacy of Latin American intellectuals. According to him, the dynamism and the opportunity to exercize leadership afforded by Marxist activism is in sharp contrast to their reduced power in the real society where the army, church, landowner, industrialist, working class labor leader and peasant organizer are, in fact, the powerful contenders for national attention. Whatever the case may be, the discovery of strong links between the Regaldo murder and the university was, to many Salvadorans, simply the final straw of a series of peculiar crises which had been building at that institution.

During the 1960s the National University grew. Alastair White points out that the governments of this period felt that ". . . if the revolutionaries are not interfered with in their own territory, and are enabled to live more comfortably, they are not so likely to make revolution." Thus, university autonomy, as well as building construction, a quadrupling of the budget, and roughly a doubling of enrollments took place. However, the revolutionary atmosphere at the University of El Salvador increasingly induced parents who could afford it or who could get scholarships (and there are many more of these than is commonly assumed) to send their children abroad — to the United States, Spain, Chile, Mexico, or Costa Rica.

Primary and secondary schools in Latin America and in El Salvador are class-based. The "better" the school, the higher the socio-economic background of its students. So, too, public universities are often disproportionately lower-middle and even working class, although anyone able to go as far as the university is, be definition, somewhat privileged. An interesting incident helps to illustrate how politicized El Salvador's universities have become. In 1964 university rector Fabio Castillo, probably the best known politician of the left and presidential candidate for the Partido Acción Renovadora (PAR) in 1967, flew to Moscow. He invited two Russian scientists to teach in El Salvador. The two lecturers from Lomonosov University were denied visas, and a big national controversy over the matter culminated in the "Great Debate" between Castillo and Interior Minister Colonel Sanchez Hernandez. On television, they fleshed out the dimensions of this problem. The government won, and to underscore its point, also denied visas to two Chileans hired by the University. Chile had always been a hotbed of Marxism and in fact Salvadoran revolutionary Cayetano Carpio spent some time there.

The cynicism of Salvadorans toward their university is highlighted by a humorous article cited by White in which the periodical *El Mundo* on December 15, 1970, mused that Communists ". . . succumb better to money than bullets. In Guatemala the anti-guerrilla struggle costs . . . approximately 50 thousand dollars a day, or an annual cost of more than 18 million dollars, plus blood. The University of El Salvador costs approximately six million dollars a year, and there the communists fight among themselves."

White also correctly designated the University of El Salvador as functionally equivalent to a political party. His description of the university is a vitally important setting from which we can proceed to analyze the fast unravelling of Salvadoran political institutions in the mid-1970s. White wrote that:

> The university acts not only as the main cultural and educational centre but also as another opposition party, one which cannot be proscribed; it has even been said that it is the only real opposition. The General Association of Salvadoran University students has played a major role in organizing protests, demonstrations and riots against the government. It also sponsors satirical parades during which every institution in the country is subjected to irreverent criticism, often couched with sexual undertones.

Student uprisings at the Sorbonne in Paris, the violence on American campuses culminating in the takeover of Columbia University by the Students for a Democratic Society (from which the violent Weathermen Underground later splintered), the growing disenchantment with the U.S. struggle against the communists in Southeast Asia, "hippy" and "yippy" movements, growing drug use (especially marijuana, heroin, LSD, and cocaine), the sexual revolution, and the advent of "free love," were all part of the tidal wave of symbols associated with university life in the late 1960s. Moreover, the cult of Cuban-Argentine revolutionary Ernesto "Che" Guevara, whose picture adorned not only student apartments but many a classroom hallway, faculty office, and even the desk of university administrators, was an ominous condition in the eyes of many. Coupled with the Regaldo murder, it added up to a very volatile mixture indeed.

Of greatest significance for our analysis is the identification of all these symbols of "leftism" with certain political parties, candidates, and movements. Of course, outright communist or Marxist political parties were suspect; often they were banned and illegal. But even more ambiguous movements such as the Christian Democrats and the PAR in El Salvador came under deep suspicion of undermining the basic traditions and fibers of order, probity, and stability.

The Partido Acción Renovadora, as we saw earlier, was the longest continually organized party in the country. As it slowly moved left over the decades, it became identified with reform issues. Its 1967 platform advocated land reform to be carried out in two years. All land over 150 manzanas would be expropriated. Plots of 6 manzanas would be distributed to farmers. Large farms such as coffee or cotton plantations would be organized into "economic associations" run by managers so that large unit productivity would remain intact though under cooperative ownership. A welfare state of unprecedented scale would be established, with massive public works to absorb the unemployed. All rent on homes was to be reduced by 40 per cent and price controls and price rollbacks of vital necessities such as medicine enforced. Taxes would be made much more progressive to soak the rich, destroy their political and economic power and give the government revenues. Money for housing would be increased and slums improved, among other things, by giving people titles to the property on which they built their shacks. Finally, diplomatic relations would be established with Socialist countries.

The Christian Democratic Party was, at this same time, struggling to walk the thin, high wire of political legitimacy. Its proposals for moderate land reform, improvements in the quality of life through government spending, tax adjustments (taxing coffee production as income), political union in Central America, and legalized rural unionization, were moderate. Christian Democratic leaders now admit that the degree of "moderation" was tactical; they wanted to be more radical but felt that the powers in control, including the military, would crush them completely if they moved farther left. In retrospect, it does not seem to have made much of a difference.

The tie-in between radical university elements, including Christian Democratic student groups, along with the Regaldo murder, sealed the fate of many left-of-center parties and leaders. Conservative Salvadorans have not forgotten that in late 1931 Alfonso Luna and Mario Zapata, associates of Farabundo Marti, published the *Red Star*, a newspaper about the Marxist group of the University of El Salvador and organ of the University Revolutionary Group. This university cell was part of the 1932 Marxist peasant uprising which cost so many lives and carries such heavy symbolic weight in El Salvador.

Salvadoran elite and middle class members reached the same conclusion as the Chileans. Christian Democrats may be well-meaning, they argued, but their policies simply lay the groundwork for communism. Moreover, moderate Christian Democrats are only one faction in a political party which tends to have a moderate and an extreme left-wing. In the end, the extreme left wing faction will win. One Chilean development which greatly frightened Salvadoran conservatives was the fragmentation of Chile's party into a group backing moderate Eduardo Frei and a radical wing associated with the "Plan Chonchol." These two factions had struggled fiercely in the late 1960s. The Chonchol plan, named after an important young factional leader of the party, Jaques Chonchol, was called "Propositions for Policy Action in the Period 1967-70 for a Non-Capitalist Way of Development." While Frei regained control of his party, his presidency of Chile (1964-1970) was marred by a tug of war between his government and socialists, communists, and radical Christian Democrats on the left and the National Party, the military, conservative business and industry, and others who feared or frowned on the apparently inevitable Chilean slide towards communism.

Anyone familiar with Salvadoran politics in the early 1970s will not underestimate the impressionability of that country to events unfolding in Chile. As the 1970 presidential election approached in Chile, the country began to rock under a surging wave of violence. President Frei declared a state of emergency and moved troops into Nuble Province on January 31, after farm workers declared a strike and demanded the expropriation and redistribution of large farms and cattle ranches. The mood in Chile on the eve of the election of its first Marxist president is extremely illuminating because it appears to have served as the model on which many Salvadorans, left and right, later patterned their strategy in the 1970s.

When Allende was elected president by Chile's parliament, conservative groups all over Latin America concluded that ". . . even when the popular vote doesn't go Marxist, the Christian Democrats will." Eduardo Frei's "Revolution in Liberty," "Integral Humanism," and his moderate nationalist and "humanistic Christian" experiment had failed in Chile. Even his own party's candidate Rodomiro Tomic Romero had, by the end of the campaign, taken an increasingly leftist, Marxist position which made him practically indistinguishable from Allende's leftist coalition. As a result, middle class and conservative Salvadorans became convinced that politics is a dichotomous process — either left or right. A "center" group such as Frei's Christian Democrats, they contended, will eventually have to make up its mind and decide whether it is capitalist and Christian, or Marxist and socialist. It must move either right or left.

The important 1972 presidential election in El Salvador

must be understood within the context of the two major events of the past two decades — the Cuban Revolution and the advent of a communist government, and the election of Salvador Allende in Chile. All of the political groups and ideological "lines" in El Salvador took their cues from these two events. It should be remembered that in 1970 President Sanchez Hernandez had pushed El Salvador into increasingly progressive reforms. The opposition of the traditional oligarchy to these reforms continued to build. More and more contacts were made inside the military and among retired army officers. The paramilitary group ORDEN (founded in 1964 or 1965) was more and more important as a counterweight to the reformist drift of the armed forces. Clearly, the 1972 election was a watershed of tremendous importance in Salvadoran political development. It was to be the last chance to continue a process of somewhat unstable, progressive, and competitive politics.

I have discussed in this chapter the events which converged in 1970 and early 1971. These established the direction and depth of political cleavages in the subsequent ten years.

Allende's victory in Chile, coming only a decade after Castro's victory in Cuba, seemed to confirm the creeping drift leftward in all of Latin America. The Regalado murder, coupled with a radicalization of Salvadoran university and intellectual life, was a further omen of the inexorable communization of society. That assassination signaled a new phase in Salvadoran violence. It would now include more and more members of politically prominent and powerful groups. Finally, in the eyes of Salvadoran conservatives and members of the armed forces, this period was seen as a time when political parties — Christian Democrats and adherents of the ideology of the PAR in particular — were moving farther to the left. As a result, the government's ability to control election outcomes slipped, and it seemed that opposition groups would finally gain ascendency through the ballot box. The "Chilean theory" stating that Christian Democrats, no matter how benign, are simply a "caretaker" party between the traditional system and communism came into vogue. It was thought that if anything could be learned from the Chilean case, it was that one needs to nip the leftward slide in the bud.

Progressive groups, mainly the Christian Democrats, believed they could attain political victory by creating alliances among leftist groups and striking a moderately reformist position between strict communism and the old order. The 1972 election and its aftermath were to become the empirical test of these hypothetical lessons.

7

Breakdown:
The End of Civil
Politics in the 1970s

By the 1970s El Salvador's political system had become a complex kaleidoscope reflecting various political factions, each promising the poor a utopia. "We were all outdoing each other to offer manna from heaven even though there was precious little manna to go around," Sergio Andrade observed.

The legendary ruling class had lost its force and vitality. Guns and walkie-talkies replaced the plush furnishings of elegant living rooms. Well-to-do families stopped coverage of their daughters' fifteenth birthday parties and notices of their trips to Europe or to the United States. The new political factions relentlessly pushed for their reforms, making very modest concessions to others. The political storm brewed — ominous clouds formed over the ruling government as the struggle for power by various factions sounded in thunderous clashes of violence drawing world attention to El Salvador.

In 1972 the government party (PCN) nearly lost the presidential election. Webre observed that this almost happened for two reasons. "After a serious reversal in 1970, the leading opposition party - the Christian Democrats - ". . . overcame their long-standing objection to coalitions and successfully organized the often progressive parties into a single front." Secondly, a large number of conservatives and rightists, who saw their interests undermined by reformist policies, began to abandon the National Conciliation Party, forming or joining right-wing splinter groups.

Two years earlier, in the 1970 elections, it had been a different story. The government party had swept control over 252 of the 261 municipal councils. Both the conservatives (PPS) and the Christian Democrats (PDC) had lost substantial control at the local level. The PDC, which controlled 78 municipalities from 1968-1970, was left with only eight, including San Salvador. The PDC fared better in assembly races, losing three of their nineteen seats. However, the official party controlled thirty-four seats, leaving one each for UDN and PPS.

As in most Latin American elections, fraud was charged as a result of many electoral irregularities. However, the role the PCN played in vindicating Salvadoran honor against Honduras in the "soccer war" played a major role in the outcome. Moreover, the policies of the incumbent administration enjoyed popular support. During the campaign, Dr. Abraham Rodriguez of the Christian Democratic Party criticized the government's role in the war with Honduras. His party was labelled anti-patriotic. Also, the PCN was in power, and used the full advantages of an incumbent administration to hold on to that power.

The PCN's use of its power left the Christian Democrats and the conservative parties weakened. Many were surprised by the actual damage suffered. Both parties promptly changed their strategy, using the 1972 election as proving ground. The Christian Democrats joined two left of center groups forming a broad front alliance. They re-evaluated their economic position and social programs, hoping to win the 1972 elections by presenting themselves as a more progressive coalition. The conservatives were in disarray. There were rumors that they had begun conspiring to overthrow the government.

Meanwhile, President Sanchez Hernandez proceeded with substantial reforms, considering El Salvador's current problems. Education Minister Walter Beneke Medina effected educational reforms. In spite of limited funds, Medina established a program calling for the construction of one new school a day. But this program failed to adequately compensate the teachers, and in 1971, they struck for two months over salaries.

One observer noted, "If this had been a socialist system, the teachers would have been told in no uncertain terms that it was their social obligation as Marxist revolutionaries to work more hours for less pay."

The author, Ronald McDonald, described the El Salvador of the 1970s as being in the process of institutionalizing the development process. Some features were ". . . changes in the electoral machinery, the emergence of more permissive electoral laws, the growth of electoral impartiality, and the extension of party organization on a permanent rather than an ad hoc basis."

Thus the 1972 election was the culmination of a gradual process through which electoral blocks and moderate reform policies gained ground. The period immediately prior to the election and the 1970 election as well, were merely moratoriums on the growing internal dissent, disruption and crisis. It appears that this was not a permanent, moderate consensus. Rather, it was a respite from the accelerating forces of leftism and radicalism on the one hand, and rightist reactionary defense of the traditional order and anti-communism on the other.

Events leading to the 1972 election spun a web of violence, official maneuvers to disqualify candidates and parties and acts of terrorism. There was also the usual practice of rural mobilization of voters by *patrones,* political bosses, power brokers and members of the armed forces and the National Guard. The extreme left — which had always repudiated elections as a burgeois trick to disguise oppression — relished the heat and vilification stirred by the pending election. The moderate left felt that combining its forces gave it a good chance to win.

The 1972 presidential election pitted Armando Molina, of the National Conciliation party, against Christian Democrat José Napoleón Duarte, who ran for the Union Nacional Opositora (UNO). The UNO included two smaller leftist parties; the Movement for National Revolution (MNR) and the National Democratic Union. Antonio Rodriguez Porth headed the ticket of the small right-wing Popular Salvadoran Party and General Jose Alberto Medrano represented the Independent United Democratic Front.

The voting was completed on February 20, 1972. Allegations of fraud and intimidation circulated, especially in the rural areas. When the ballots were counted, no candidate had gained an absolute majority so the election was thrown into the National Assembly. On February 25, Molina was declared winner. The National Assembly decided this on the basis of Molina's 10,000 vote majority over the next highest group, the Christian Democrats. Candidate Duarte alleged fraud. Prior to the balloting, Medrano boycotted the elections, feeling that the "public will again be mocked by the government." Earlier, Medrano had declared ". . . if the government party wins the elections, there will be a coup d'etat. The government party is corrupt and the armed forces do not like corruption."

Following the election, congressional and local seats were allocated: the PCN was given 38 of 52 seats in Congress and 206 of 261 mayoralities; the UNO was awarded seven

congressional seats and 54 mayoralities; the PPS received six
seats in Congress and one mayorality, while the Independent
United Democratic Front got one Congressional seat. But
all these allocations were to prove academic. In March 1972,
the extreme left, after repudiating the electoral participation
of the UNO and left groups, launched a series of attacks against
the National Guard. Arson broke out in the capital city. Government agents raided the university, turning up caches of arms
and communist pamphlets. On March 20, 1972, the body of
UNO councilman Alvayero, from San Marcos, was found in a
ditch on a deserted stretch of road. The National Guard had
arrested him a short while earlier. The left promptly accused the
government of murder and intimidation. The atmosphere in
the nation, particularly in San Salvador, was electric. A crisis
clearly was building.

The early morning hours of March 25, 1972 opened to
the sound of gunfire throughout San Salvador. An artillery
officer, Colonel Benjamin Mejia, was leading an attempt to
overthrow the government. As commander of the Zapote
barracks in the capital, Mejia counted on army troops and
"military youth" to ensure his victory. He ordered the seizure
of President Sanchez Hernandez. But Colonel Mejia had not
counted on the Salvadoran Air Force, which remained loyal
to the government. Within a few hours aircraft had begun to
bomb the rebel installations. There were others not siding with
the colonel, including the National Guard, the National Police
and the Treasury Police. Their commanders called for rein-
forcements, and soon other supporters of the government
began to stream into San Salvador from outlying regions.

Rumors abounded throughout the streets and cafes of the
capital city. Some said that Napoleón Duarte was behind the
coup because he had wanted to set up a progressive government.
He felt that this had been denied him by the fraudulent election. Others speculated that General Medrano was the culprit.
Every non-government faction in fact was suspect and accused

by someone.

In truth it appears that Colonel Mejia and his second-in-command, Colonel Nuñez, were really attempting nothing more than a classic military coup d'etat, seeking power to aid their own personal ambitions. After learning of the coup in the early morning hours of March 25, José Napoleón Duarte spoke over the radio, counseling troops to reject the Mejia order and remain loyal to the government. Partially because of Duarte's speech and partially because of mismanagement, the coup of Colonel Mejia failed. Soon the government was in full control of the city.

Even though he was vocal in his allegiance to the government, José Duarte did not escape the repression which quickly followed on the heels of the violence. Hearing that they were suspect, Duarte and other non-government leaders scurried to foreign embassies where they sought political asylum. Duarte was dragged by the police from the home of the First Secretary of the Venezuelan Embassy. He was beaten and taken into custody. Later he and other non-government political leaders were flown out of the country, Duarte spending his exile in Caracas, Venezuela.

Once Molina had finally taken office, tensions actually increased rather than subsided. On July 19, the army occupied the university grounds and buildings. The Rector, Dr. Rafael Menjivar, and five other regents were arrested, then exiled to Nicaragua. The government claimed that a university under communist influence and control was not in the national interest. Evidence was given that students and some professors had used the university as a center for planning robberies and kidnappings and as a base for distributing subversive literature. There were also allegations that the university was a known hotbed for the local drug culture and those engaged in "sexual abuses." Among the more spectacular revelations was the discovery of secret cellars and tunnels in which the police allegedly found automobiles fitting the description of those used in recent bank robberies. The government further charged that an audit of the university's financial books revealed that officials had used a scholarship fund to secretly send students to Prague, Moscow and Havana. In an attempt to purge the teaching staff, 37 foreign-born professors were fired and expelled from El Salvador.

During the first year of the Molina administration, the government tried the coup leaders in absentia. Duarte was cleared of all charges. Others, including Colonel Mejia, were sentenced to prison terms, even though all had been either exiled or had fled the country.

The crisis that was to form over the next few years had already begun in 1973. On February 16, the government reported the discovery of an "international terrorist plot" led by the Salvadoran Communist Party. More than one hundred left wing labor leaders and politicians were arrested. Many were exiled to Guatemala. Communist party leader Jacinto Castellanos was arrested on March 13 for carrying $50,000 in cash, which the government suspected would be used to finance the plot.

Anxious to obtain Mexican private investments in El Salvador, President Molina denied charges that his social and economic program was socialist — a curious allegation against a government so strongly opposed by the left. However, it should be noted that conservatives went so far as to call Molina's regime "communist."

In addition to political problems, the Salvadoran economy reeled under a thirty to forty per cent reduction in the sale of coffee, the country's major export commodity. A serious drought brought on the rationing of water, limiting it to an hour-a-day use in most cities. There was also a sharp drop in the supply of maize, rice and beans. Sporadic acts of violence occurred, including the bombing of an army barracks in Santa Anna and the massive bombing of an IBM office. The Popular Liberation Front claimed responsibility for the IBM bombing of May 11, which caused half a million dollars damage. Charges of government human rights violations were heard as security forces searched for the terrorists. These events, and the prospect of long-term security problems with both Honduras and domestic revolutionary groups, led to the September arms deal with Israel, in which 25 jet fighters were ordered. As with most governments of its type, the Molina administration tried to balance its controversial law and order position by putting moderates in the cabinet, a strategy successfully followed by most Salvadoran regimes. However, toward the end of 1973 Economy Minister Salvador Sanchez and Agriculture Minister Enrique Alvarez resigned.

In February of 1974, the new Agriculture Minister Roberto Llach Hill (a member of one of the "old" families) and his deputy resigned, primarily because the Molina administration was bowing before powerful agricultural interests and backing away from land reform programs. It should be emphasized that resignations of moderates have a powerful weakening effect on a government whose legitimacy is barely acceptable. Sweeping Congressional and mayoral victories in 1974 further undermined the government's position when the opposition charged fraud.

Meanwhile, the left began to refine and intensify its use of guerrilla attacks on the government. On February 27, a bomb exploded outside the police station in Chachualpa. On March 3, members of the "People's Revolutionary Army" seized two radio stations in San Salvador, broadcasting revolutionary messages. Three days later, guerrillas attacked the National Elections Council and two soldiers defending the offices were killed. These acts, preceeding the March 10 elections, underscored the contempt opposition groups, including the extreme left, felt toward elections in El Salvador. Usually elections lend credibility to a government, but hostility had developed toward elections due to fraud and the fact that rural, illiterate people did not know how to use the ballot as an instrument to improve their lives.

In the disputed 1974 elections, the PCN won 32 legislative seats, the UNO 14, the PPS four and the United Independent Democratic Front two. The PCN won most mayoralities, although San Salvador remained in the hands of the Christian Democrats. These positions, though secured through elections, were viewed by the opposition as fraudulent and coersive products of the government. Bombings and guerrilla attacks rose in late 1975 after the government announced plans for elections to be held on March 14, 1976. In these anti-election raids, dozens of people were wounded and four security officers were killed. These occurrences were only an afterthought compared to the increase in mass demonstrations and the terrorist assaults used by leftists in 1975.

On July 19, 1975, in an effort to attract long-term tourism, a million dollar investment brought the "Miss Universe" pageant to San Salvador. Salvadoran revolutionaries used the publicity the pageant brought to draw attention to the repressive government, just as Mexican students had used the Olympics to attract attention to their cause. The government labelled the riots a "communist conspiracy." Twelve students were killed and many more injured, but the student and farm groups claimed they had no alternative to violence.

The see-saw of unrest pounded at a deafening, violent tempo. When peasants organized and began to voice their demands, government and para-military forces terrorized them. There were allegations of government massacres in the villages of La Cayetana and Tres Calles. The charges were denied. On August 1, a group of students, peasants, workers and priests occupied the metropolitan cathedral in San Salvador, issuing a list of demands. These demands included compensation to the families of those killed in riots, the resignation of Defense Minister Carlos Humberto Romero, and the release of all political prisoners. The La Cayetana murders — where over 50 peasants were said to have been killed — was an especially critical issue. Its urgency drew the nation's Roman Catholic

Bishops to the forefront of political unrest. New revolutionary groups formed when security forces blindly struck out against increasing government opposition.

A new breed of terrorist emerged in El Salvador. One such group was the People's Revolutionary Army (ERP). The ERP kidnapped wealthy industrialist Francisco Sola, collecting two million dollars ransom, then issued a pamphlet calling the ransom "a war tax for the Salvadoran revolution." The technique of raising funds through abduction and bank robbery became a powerful tool in financing revolutionary activity, and was widely used by leftist groups. But the ferocity of ERP was most clearly evident when it executed a well-known communist writer named Roque Dalton Garcia for his supposed treachery and disagreement with "guerrillas." Garcia was believed to have opposed the strategy of terrorism for which the ERP was laying the groundwork.

A second group, the Worker's Revolutionary Organization made its major debut with a powerful bomb explosion at the National Tourist Institute. A number of explosions at the National University were also attributed to the WRO. As violence escalated, workers and others hard hit by the country's depressed economy were mobilized by the leftist and communist organizations. Strikes and demonstrations by these groups represented a different, but debilitating dimension of pressure on the Molina government.

Early in 1976, Freedom House — the New York based nonpartisan, nonprofit organization — issued a report. It concluded that of all the Latin American Nations only Venezuela, Colombia, Surinam, El Salvador and Costa Rica were democratic. We shall not attempt to evaluate Freedom House's criteria as applied to El Salvador. However, it seems peculiar that El Salvador should be ranked with only four other Latin American countries when domestic opposition groups there condemned the government as a repressive illegal dictatorship.

On March 14, 1976, elections were held despite threats

from the left. The major opposition of UNO denied the government a symbolic victory. UNO withdrew from the elections and the *oficilista* PCN won all 54 deputy seats and all 261 mayoralities. Prior to the election the government made every effort to disqualify UNO candidates. President Molina charged that UNO was taking both money and instructions from abroad and that this came from "international communists" and "false Christians." The ERP set off bombs to protest the upcoming election. PCN headquarters and other offices were particularly hard hit. At the same time ERP was undergoing reorganization. In the fifth or sixth split since its founding, the group again, in early April, executed one of its dissenting leaders. In turn, each of the splinter groups of ERP formed new revolutionary military organizations.

What was occurring in El Salvador's rural areas during this period is still unclear. Press reports and observer's accounts are few, but fragmentary evidence indicates that the rural areas were slowly being radicalized. The peasants, store owners, petty politicians and small-time bosses were the unpublicized victims of radicalization of the 1970s. These Salvadorans were shot and dumped along roadsides or tortured for information about communists.

Inside the armed forces, this was a period of soul-searching and of evaluating one's political alignment — left, right, center, or apolitical. Caught in the tide of political change, the armed forces leaders felt increasingly uncomfortable with the role they were playing. The Treasury and Cantonal Police, the National Guard, the Federal Police and the para-military ORDEN were heavily involved in these political battles. By 1976 the regular armed forces were engulfed in the violence as well.

Added to the violence was the ignominious Rodriguez affair. On May 15, in a Mount Kisco, New York Motel, Col. Manuel Alfonso Rodriguez was arrested by U.S. Treasury agents. Col. Rodriguez, El Salvador's armed forces chief of staff, and six co-defendents (one Salvadoran and five Americans) were caught in a sting operation. Joseph F. Kelly, a special agent of the U.S. Treasury's Department of Alcohol, Tobacco and Firearms, and several other agents, had posed as underworld crime figures interested in buying arms. Rodriguez had put in an order to the State Department for ten thousand submachine guns to be used for "the national defense of El Salvador". The guns, which were to be sold for $2.8 million dollars, were to be part of an even bigger future deal. On November 23, in a U.S. District Court in Manhattan, Col. Rodriguez was sentenced to ten years in prison. This incident caused deep embarrassment and shock among professional officers in the Salvadoran armed forces. A number of younger officers were dismayed and resentful of this military corruption at the highest echelons.

By December 22, when the *New York Times* published the annual survey of Freedom House for the year 1976, El Salvador had fallen from "free" to "partly free." "Not free," the lowest category, was held by such Latin American countries as Argentina, Paraguay and Uruguay.

The next phase in Salvadoran politics centered on the new president elected in March 1977. Col. Carlos Humberto Romero had resigned as Minister of Defense and had been nominated as the presidential candidate of the ruling National Conciliation Party in July. As expected, Romero, a hard-line conservative, won the 1977 presidential election over Col. Ernesto Claramount Rozeville and his Christian Democratic Party running mate, Jose Antonio Morales Ehrlich. The election was widely reputed to have been fixed.

The pattern was classic. Ronald McDonald observed that "the post-1948 military regimes have been plagued by fundamental contradictions, which increasingly have eroded their capability to govern. The regimes have presented themselves as revolutionary, when in fact, they are not. They have tried to implant in their nation a concept of government borrowed from Mexico, which is incongruent. They have paid lip service to the basic elements of democracy and gone long distances to give the appearance of democratic process, yet the country has been wholly under the control of a military institution that is unwilling to surrender power to any other group. They have acknowledged the inequities and injustices of their society, but for whatever reasons — many possibly beyond their control — they have done little if anything to diminish them."

McDonald further argued that the military had recognized that the ruling oligarchy was not adapting to El Salvador's problems.   The charges of fraud resulted in demonstrations and a general strike on February 20, 1977.   On February 28, at least six people died and dozens were wounded in shootouts during demonstrations in San Salvador. A thirty-day state of siege was declared. Claramount went into exile.

Concern over deteriorating conditions and the newly inaugurated Carter administration's resolve to make human rights its cornerstone prompted congressional hearings on March 7 and March 17 in Washington, D.C.. The subcommittee on International Relations concluded that no "clear pattern" of human rights violations could be established. Therefore, security assistance was not suspended as provided by Section 502B of the 1961 U.S. Foreign Assistance Act. However, the hearings alone were interpreted as a criticism of the Salvadoran government. El Salvador's defense minister renounced the American military aid program on March 16 and ordered troops who were being trained in the United States to come home.

Under conservative pressure, the Romero government showed signs of scrapping the pending land reform program. The leftist Farabundo Marti Popular Liberation Front opened its offensive by kidnapping Foreign Minister Mauricio Borgonovo Pohl. The Liberation Front demanded release of 36 political prisoners. No concessions were made and Pohl was killed.

A rightist group, the White Warriors Union, took revenge by killing a Roman Catholic priest. On May 19 government troops and members of the Christian Federation of Salvadoran Peasants — a group pressing for land reform — clashed. Seven people died. Archbishop Romero and six other bishops accused the government of systematic persecution of the church priests. As in most of Latin America, the church was fragmented between conservatives and reform-oriented clergy. Moreover, right wing forces increasingly viewed church members as "communist."

As a result of the violence, particularly the persecution of church members, the Carter administration withdrew its support of a 90 million dollar Inter-American Development Bank loan to El Salvador. However, by October 1977 the administration did an about-face and requested the funds. But the Carter administration continued to exert pressure on behalf of human rights in July when it held up all U.S. arms sales to El Salvador.

In 1977 the Guerrilla Army of the Poor kidnapped El Salvador's ambassador to Guatemala, Col. Eduardo Casanova Sandoval. The kidnappers demanded that an anti-capitalist statement be read at the Inter-American Development Bank's annual meeting, then being held in Guatemala. The demand was complied with and Ambassador Casanova was freed. The Guerrilla Army had been linked to the organization that killed Salvadoran Foreign Minister Borgonovo Pohl in April. U.S. Ambassador Ignacio Lozano asked in vain for an investigation into the disappearance of an American citizen, Ronald J. Richardson, from an El Salvador jail. It was feared that Richardson had been killed by security forces. Increased brutality and threats against Jesuit priests encouraged San Salvador's Archbishop Oscar Romero to speak vehemently against violence. The archbishop boycotted the Romero Presidential inauguration and vigorously spoke of the need for social change at the same time demanding protection for the Catholic clergy.

American Ambassador Lozano complained to the government and exerted local pressure to improve human rights. But in July and August of 1977 very little direction came from Washington. Both the escalating mortality — what the U.S. human rights activists have called the "charnel house atmosphere" — and the Carter administration's ambivalence about what to do resulted in disarray in U.S.-Salvadoran relations. Friendly gestures from the new Romero government received a cold shoulder from Washington. In September, amid confusion and tension, terrorists struck again, machine gunning Carlos Alfaro Castillo, rector of El Salvador University. Increasing violence against peasants in rural areas was reported. In mid-October, the U.S. Senate approved a bill barring some forms of military aid to El Salvador. All in all, 1977 was a tragic year in the history of El Salvador.

The March 1978 elections for assembly deputies and municipal councilmen were again boycotted by all parties except the government National Conciliation Party (PCN).

The Salvadoran situation worsened, and 1979 clearly stands as the turning point. In January, Fritz Schuitema, a Phillips' executive, was released unharmed by kidnappers after four million dollars was paid in ransom. This was only one of dozens of kidnappings and seizures of buildings by leftists and peasant-farmer groups. The Organization of American States offices were occupied by dissidents and the Mexican Embassy was seized.

A damaging report by the Inter-American Human Rights Commission accused El Salvador's government of murdering political opponents and committing acts of torture. The committee recommended that the 80,000 man paramilitary force, ORDEN, be dismantled because it was responsible for the repression of peasants. The left and right continued to match each other in violence. In February, the Revolutionary Army of the Poor bombed the central police headquarters in San Salvador, along with two police stations. Twenty died and dozens were injured. A strike by electrical workers virtually paralyzed the country. In April, heavily armed leftists seized the French and Costa Rican Embassies, taking thirty hostages and killing three security officers near these buildings. In May the Venezuelan Embassy was taken. Later two policemen died warding off an attack on the South African Embassy.

Swiss charge d'affaires Hugo Wey was shot to death by four youths who tried to abduct him from his automobile. Three foreign executives, the Bank of London's Ian Massie and Michael Chatterton, and Japanese businessman Tatakazu Suzuki, were kidnapped and held in exchange for release of five political prisoners, the publication of a political manifesto, and forty million dollars. A fourth captive, prominent Salvadoran coffee trader Ernesto Liebes, was found dead. Demonstrations were held almost weekly against the violence, or on behalf of reform or revolution. Security forces frequently fired into the crowds, and reports of leftist snipers abounded. Many died and were injured in the chaos. Leftists retaliated with bombings and the killing of policemen and soldiers. The Popular Revolutionary Bloc, a Marxist-Leninst group, emerged as the most aggressive element on the left and took responsibility for most of the urban violence. In May, Education Minister Carlos Antonio Herrera Rebollo and his chauffeur were assassinated. The Farabundo Marti Popular Liberation Forces claimed responsibility. That same group took credit for the machine gun killing of Army Major Armando de Paz as he drove to his office in the Defense Ministry.

President Romero unsuccessfully attempted to organize a forum to explore ways to end the violence. He blamed "international subversives" who were interfering in El Salvador's internal affairs. An influential retired general and former presidential candidate, José Alberto Medrano, accused the government of contributing to the crisis by "abusing its constitutional power." In September José Javier Romero Mena, the president's older brother, was killed by four masked gunmen. Two American businessmen, Dennis McDonald and

Fausto Buchelli, were abducted. Their employer, Bechman Instruments, responded to the kidnappers' demands, paying for the publication of a revolutionary manifesto issued on behalf of the Revolutionary Party of Central American Workers in various United States, Latin American and European newspapers. Violence in the rural areas, though little-reported, continued on a wide scale. Some 6,000 dead were reported nationwide. Many foreign businesses closed down their Salvadoran operations. Salvadorans themselves began moving their assets outside the country. Investments dwindled. Jobs disappeared. The Salvadoran economy ground down to a virtual standstill.

In sum, the decade of the 1970s began on a bright note and ended in disaster. The 1970 election proved to be the high point for the *oficialista* party, the PCN. Nationalist feelings over the Honduran War were running high, and land reform programs were popularly supported. Also a relative state of internal freedom existed, contributing to the PCN's popularity. Various conservative groups still placed their faith in the PCN, while the forces of the extreme left were split and fragmented. Only the Christian Democrats, who had worked hard at the grass roots level, represented a growing, stable party of opposition.

However, by 1972, conditions had seriously deteriorated. A growing, unified leftist coalition, the UNO, had gained considerable popular support at the polls. The right was divided. One right-wing faction sought to build its own power base through the formation of the Popular Salvadoran Party. Others backed the Independent United Democratic Front, headed by General José Alberto Medrano, the hero of the Honduran War. By 1972 the full effects of economic problems caused in large measure by the recent war with Honduras began to be felt throughout the Salvadoran economy. Costly government programs and substantial increases in loans from external development agencies only served to worsen the economic situation. At the same time the political right was becoming increasingly restless, voicing its fears of a "Chilean trend" towards socialism, while the political left had begun shifting its tactics towards militancy and violence.

The year 1972 also began a cycle of fraudulent elections in which opposition political parties could not gain power through the ballot. Again and again the official PCN denied the UNO and other political parties representation through free elections, and few opposition party candidates were allowed positions as mayors, members of municipal councils and in the national assembly. With all legal and peaceful routes to political representation closed, the political parties sought extra-legal and even violent paths to power.

The extreme left had never viewed election as a means of achieving power. They were joined by less radical elements who had also given up on the "constitutional" process. Even more violent revolutionary groups sprang up during the 1970s. These groups were intent on setting in motion a fairly systematic process of attrition that would eventually lead to revolutionary success. They began building a war chest by kidnapping for ransom. This was followed by targeted terrorism against government personnel designed to provoke the regime into excessive retaliation. In the dramatic IBM bombing, an economic war against the government had begun, designed to frighten foreign investors and cause the flight of international companies already in the country. The revolutionaries also targeted prominent Salvadorans for terrorization, forcing them to flee the country. This caused the loss of domestic capital and the decapitalization of domestic farms, businesses, industry and banking. Finally, the extreme left attacked the very promising tourist industry, effectively putting an end to a potentially rich source of foreign exchange.

The end of 1977 marked the point at which El Salvador's business, commercial, professional and industrial community decided that they could no longer rely on the government for protection. Houses began to sprout extensions of the huge walls that surround most upper class homes in Latin America. Rolls of concertina wire laced the tops of these twenty to thirty foot high fortresses. External doors were bricked shut and heavy steel garage doors were installed. Private security guards, terrorist-proof automobiles, and personal devices such as bullet-proof vests and UZI submachine guns were in popular demand. The television security monitoring business flourished as most of the middle and upper classes became obsessed with personal safety.

Children were sent to school outside the country. The ubiquitous money launderers began to make fortunes changing *colones* into American dollars which were pumped into Costa Rican, Swiss, American and Mexican bank accounts. Businessmen stopped buying new equipment and cut inventories to the bone. Moreover, those who increasingly felt exposed to violence began to strike back. An internal war mentality definitely emerged starting in the late 1970s. Right and left wing terrorist groups operated with greater impunity, meting out "justice" and avenging acts of violence. The right intensified its effort to convince conservative elements in the security forces to "do something about the communists." A substantial number of officers in the various branches of the security organizations appear to have agreed that they needed to take strong and decisive action, whether or not it was the government's desire to do so. Private armies, death squads and anti-communist brigades all started to take root.

From a human rights, military, security, and anti-terrorism perspective the Molina and Romero governments were probably in a more complex situation than the simplistic right-left paradigm suggests. Aside from "official" policy emanating from the executive office of the president, there were innumerable "mini-policies" or at least "mini-projects" undertaken by various elements in the five or so security forces. It should be stressed that in Latin America, regional and local commanders have always exercised unusual discretion. Often they are

the ones who   issue a   *levantamiento* (uprising) against the
central government. Thus in the use of force, local commanders
and even non-commissioned officers, more often than not,
made local decisions based on a host of local circumstances,
local power structures and local or even personal value judgements or personal needs.

One Air Force officer — since killed by either leftist or
right wing terrorists — told me the following story which may
be illustrative of this personalized process going on in the
late 1970s.

> Several months ago, I was awakened by one of
> the soldiers under my command at about 3 A.M..
>
> 'Commandant,' the soldier said, 'it is urgent that
> you give us a pass for a few days. We need to take
> care of some personal business.'
>
> 'No. We are on duty and you need to wait until
> your normal free time. What is it you need to do
> that is so urgent? ' I asked the young recruit who
> was about eighteen, but looked thirteen.
>
> 'Well Commandant, compadre Tulio Lopez just
> got word from his village. An old man brought
> a message an hour ago. The communists came into
> his village and found a letter he wrote to his mother
> a few weeks ago. They took the whole family outside
> and told the villagers not to let their sons go into the
> army. Then they decapitated *compañero* Lopez's
> mother, three sisters and the old uncle from El
> Pepeto who was living with them. Then they burned
> their house. There are several of us here from the
> same town and we want to help find these killers.'
>
> 'No, you cannot go and take revenge by yourself,'
> I told him. 'The government will try to find the
> culpable people and they will be brought to justice.'
> I saw a faint, disbelieving and cynical smile on the

young soldier's face, as if he were thinking, 'Commandant, this government can't find anything anywhere and the murderers of *compañero* Lopez's family will never be brought to justice.'

'Then with respect sir, we will simply go and take the punishment you must give us for leaving the barracks without permission,' the young soldier told me. I gave them a pass. They would have deserted. These four poor young men left in the early dawn for the mountains. For three days they hunted down the people who reportedly killed Lopez's family. These are young boys who have lived, hunted and loved in those mountains and they knew every rock, every campesino, every gully. They found a small party of insurgents sleeping in their hammocks.

The next day they marched the three guerrillas back to Lopez's village. The townspeople identified them. On the very spot where the earlier execution had taken place, they decapitated the three. Then they returned to the barracks and never said a word to anyone. I found out how their mission of personal vengeance had gone from the old man who came from the village to bring another message for one of the other recruits. His father had just been abducted by the guerrillas.

I have no doubt at all that a large part of the violence which began to convulse El Salvador in the 1970s was caused by the undisciplined personal actions of people such as these soldiers. Probably this same story (except in reverse, with security forces killing villagers) has been repeated many times by the insurgent groups on the other side. I am quite sure that both President Molina and President Romero had developed a detailed "official plan" for responding to violence, to riots, kidnappings, building seizures, and terrorist attacks. That official plan may indeed have included harsh repressive measures. However, one must go beyond the official plan, whatever that was, to understand the personal manifestations of violence. This more complex analysis of violence gives a more accurate picture of reality.

Under the accelerating conditions of crisis, the Romero government found itself faced not only with internal problems but also with a new international standard by which it would be judged — the human rights policies of the Carter administration. Sadly, General Romero proved to be incapable of dealing with these internal and external pressures.

8

October 15, 1979: The Coup D'Etat and the Arrival of the "Progressive" Juntas

"As we awakened on Monday, October 15, 1979," writes former U.S. Ambassador to El Salvador, Frank Devine, "word quickly came that a military coup d'etat was underway. Early that morning, various military garrisons and forces had joined in telling President Romero that he should step down."

The coup should not have come as a surprise to the ambassador. Violence in El Salvador had intensified. The Salvadoran elite panicked at the impunity with which the left mobilized its forces. By early 1979, the situation was critical. Devine noted, "We were told that the point of no return had been passed, that President Romero's statements had lost

100

credibility, and that he was incapable of providing the moral, effective leadership to carry the nation to honest elections."

The U.S. Embassy was abuzz with speculation. In his book, *El Salvador: Embassy Under Attack*, Devine mentions three political alternatives that Salvadorans were discussing: First, ". . . a violent and bloody uprising by the poor, led and orchestrated by the extreme left." Second, ". . . elections held in a political and electoral climate that was entirely unpropitious," and third, ". . . a change of government by a coup d'etat within the military."

A fourth alternative was to maintain the status quo. Devine said the United States favored "fair and honest elections." That seems a peculiar choice, considering the historical role of elections under undemocratic governments in El Salvador during the 1970s. Also, it seems incredible to propose that "fair and honest elections" could possibly be held in such a chaotic atmosphere. The opposition viewed the elections of March 12, 1980 as another fraudulent legitimization of an unpopular government. Violence increased in 1979 as a prelude to the forthcoming March 1980 election.

Devine recounts how the United States attempted to secure guarantees for a fairer election. Devine met with President Romero and urged him to "mitigate the conflict." Supposedly, Romero smiled after the ambassador left and remarked that "the gringos had no idea how to fight communism." A few weeks earlier at a private dinner, Romero had made a similar remark with reference to America's role in Vietnam.

The ambassador also met with the opposition, asking them to ease their pressure on Romero. Their leaders scoffed at the idea, saying that Romero had had plenty of time to reduce the repression. The opposition claimed that Romero was finished, and that "some other form of change was imminent, and the United States stood in danger of missing the boat if it didn't get on board."

Next, Devine asked for the assistance of business leaders,

but they insisted that Romero had already made concessions for a free election in his August speech. In that speech Romero called for reorganization of the electoral law and a restructuring of the Electoral Council. He also encouraged political refugees to come back for the election, and invited the Organization of American States to send observers. The businessmen gave no indication that they would pressure Romero. Actually, the conservatives were no more supportive of elections than the leftists.   They feared a "Chilean-Allende" replay occurring as a result of the election.

The ambassador heard more bad news from representatives of the church. The parishioners were telling church leaders that they did not believe in elections. One church leader told Devine that elections under these circumstances were impractical, but that a violent revolution led by the extreme left was unthinkable. The church leader observed that ". . . the coup d'etat from within the military was beginning to be seen by many Salvadorans as the only feasible remaining alternative. If it were to be a coup by the right wing faction of the military, nothing would change except possibly a few names and faces. The day of reckoning would only be postponed. If the coup were to be staged by younger reform-minded officers of the military, however, there might yet be a chance for some accommodation and understanding with the people."

According to Devine, young, reform-minded officers appear to have been responsible for the coup of October 15th. It was 5:30 P.M. when the embassy heard about the overthrow.

Devine denied rumors that the U.S. Embassy and the U.S. State Department were involved in the coup. Devine's narrative does not state clearly just how involved the United States was with the Salvadoran armed forces.   It is clear that officials of the United States held extensive conversations with Salvadorans after President Carter began his campaign on behalf of human rights. The U.S. Embassy's contact with a host of Salvadoran groups gave the impression that the United

States wanted an alternative to the Romero government. It is more likely that the United States, after evaluating the five political choices — a leftist revolution, an election, a continuation of the status quo, a hard-line right-wing coup, or a left-of-center progressive coup — sent out signals that it favored the last alternative.

Paćcido Edozain, an Augustinian priest who worked with Archbishop Romero in the Archdiocese of San Salvador, provides an intriguing commentary and chronology of the downfall of General Romero's government.

> September 11, 1979 — Undersecretary of State for Inter-American Affairs presented a plan "Central America at the Crossroads" to the State Department. In it he noted that in El Salvador ". . . the possibilities of avoiding violence are quickly disappearing" and that the U.S. should accelerate aid and ". . . give support to genuine and serious reforms."

> September 14, 1979 — Carter Administration spokesman Hodding Carter said that two U.S. diplomats had suggested to General Romero that he resign from the presidency as a sign of good faith of his desire for democracy in El Salvador.

> October 10, 1979 — Carter ordered a military alert for the Caribbean and Central America after "discovering" a division of Soviet troops in Cuba. Edozain quotes Senator Stone as saying that the alert would guarantee better United States aid to Honduras, Guatemala, and El Salvador.

October 14, 1979 — General Romero took a short
trip for "health reasons" to the United States.

October 15, 1979 — "General Romero and his
toadies . . . " leave for the United States. An
in-house coup had been engineered by "young
officers." The author calls this the counter-revolutionary junta.

October 16, 1979 — The United States calls the
junta "moderate, centrist," and encouraging to
the U.S. State Department.

Whether Ambassador Devine knew of the coup is a matter
for speculation. I would argue that he was on intimate terms
with both Colonel Jaime Abdul Gutierrez, the leader of the
plot against Romero, and Colonel Arnoldo Adolfo Majano,
an engineer with the Military Academy and latecomer to the
coup. Three civilians were appointed to the junta: Mario
Andino, a moderate businessman known to be an efficient
negotiator and good administrator; Guillermo Manuel Ungo,
the Secretary General of the Socialist Party, the National
Revolutionary Movement (MNR), and a member of the loosely
organized fourteen-party Popular Forum; and Román Mayorga,
Rector of the Catholic University, a left-of-center intellectual
identified with what has been called the "Jesuit Mafia" of the
university.
    One of the first actions of the junta was to abolish the
paramilitary organization ORDEN. The junta also promised to
investigate incidents of torture, murder and abduction. The
junta planned to establish diplomatic relations with Cuba and to
strengthen ties with the Sandinistas in Nicaragua. The new

government offered anmesty to political prisoners and exiles. It also reshuffled the military command, retiring officers closely implicated with the Romero regime. The new leaders proposed presidental elections as soon as possible. And the government issued a decree prohibiting owners of more than 100 hectares of land from transferring or encumbering their property to forestall plans for a new land reform program.

In the aftermath of the coup and the establishment of the "progressive junta," the United States, both liberal and conservative, passed judgement on the new government. The Carter administration indicated that the takeover was the best alternative to the Salvadoran crisis. Devine argues that the left, after assessing the situation created by a reform junta, ". . . came to recognize displacement of the Romero administration as a serious blow to their revolutionary interests." American conservatives were clearly distressed, fearing the political slide leftward could seriously reduce the conservatives' strength, possibly resulting in a communist government for El Salvador. The leftists simply dismissed the junta as an internal device that would delay revolutionary victory.

Three other U.S. groups assessed the effect of the new government. Extreme conservatives in the U.S. Congress, such as Jesse Helms, and a number of conservative U.S. business and church groups, opposed the takeover. Liberals, on the other hand, such as Congressman Tom Harkin, and human rights and religious organizations, favored the junta.

The following hypothetical table will illustrate how each of the six major Salvadoran constituencies had a preferable and an acceptable choice concerning problems caused by the Romero government. Also, each group viewed certain alternatives as unacceptable.

Hypothetical Preferences In Dealing With The El Salvador Crisis: May 1979

	Carter Administration	Conservative Salvadoreans	Leftist Revolutionary Salvadoreans	United States Conservatives (Congress) Religious and Patriotic Groups	United States Liberals (Congress) Human Rights and Church Groups	United States Radicals (Congress) Human Rights and Church Groups
First Choice	A Progressive Reform Junta	A Tough Anti-Communist Rightist Junta	A Victory For The Progressive Revolutionary Groups	Toughing It Out Until an Election With Conservative Victory Could Be Held	Progressive Junta	Allow People's Revolution To Succeed
Second Choice	Try to Hold An Election To Replace Romero	Replace Romero In Election With Even Tougher Conservative	A Right-Wing Coup Which Would "Show Its Hand As A Dictatorship" Even More Than Romero	A Rightest Coup	A Progressive Revolution From The Moderate Left	No Choice
Unacceptable	Right-Wing Coup	.Leftist Revolution .Progressive Junta	.Progressive Junta .Elections	.Progressive Junta .Leftist Revolution	Rightist Coup	.Progressive Junta .Election .Rightist Coup

The table clearly shows that all important political sectors had irreconcilable differences concerning preferences and unacceptable alternatives. It was not an oversight that I did not include a category of "center political groups in El Salvador." Such a category was not included because in late 1979 there was no functioning center party movement. Civilian moderates were forced to choose between the rising revolutionary movement or the military. Not one of these groups appealed to the moderates, since none promised to preserve the electoral and representative process. This lack of appeal is apparent in countries such as Cuba, where there are no political parties. Revolutionary groups also do not effectively participate in the political systems in countries such as Chile and Uruguay.

A frantic power struggle developed soon after Romero left the country. A frenzy of speculation occurred in damp military barracks over tin plates of beans, rice, an occasional chunk of hot *tamal*, and watery sweet coffee. How far left would the junta go? Would they become El Salvador's Sandinistas and turn power over to a leftist revolutionary command? Would the regular military and all the security forces be disbanded, their leaders tried, or exiled, as some officers feared? Would the United States support the new government? Or was the takeover just a cosmetic change to prevent a leftist victory? Would the increasingly outspoken union leaders, peasant, church and student groups be accepted by this new government? Or would this government act against subversives, as the Romero regime had? Could any military man possibly trust junta leaders Ungo and Mayorga, who clearly sympathized with a socialist-revolutionary government and who influenced thousands of terrorists in every town, ravine and forest?

After the coup, double scotch and sodas were served in unprecedented numbers in the Ambassador Room of the Hotel Terraza. Waiters in starched white jackets rushed platters of giant shrimp sautéed in *chicha* (hard cider), well-done steaks, and snack trays of *pupusas* (corn cakes stuffed with cream cheese and other fillings) to crowded tables of businessmen, professionals and ranchers. The questions that were being asked in the military barracks were being asked here, too. Many of the diners in the Ambassador Room were contemptuous of the "weak-bellied" U.S. Embassy and a "naive" Jimmy Carter. They believed that U.S. policy and support of the new government left Latin America wide open to a communist takeover. These feelings gave many of the diners indigestion. Meanwhile, the band played songs at the side of the pool where children played. Elegantly dressed wives and young ladies wondered if they would have to leave for Guatemala, Costa Rica or San Francisco, "for their children's safety if things went on like this."

The beleaguered Salvadoran clergy also met to review the brutality, martyrdom and suffering which it had endured and shared with the Salvadoran poor. Earnest men in short-sleeved white shirts, undershirts peeking out of the top of the open collars, dark-rimmed, square glasses and slicked-back hair met around the semicircular tables in Domus Mariae.

These men sitting on folding chairs looked at each other's papers, briefcases and cups of water, not daring to hope that this junta could end the bloody violence. The men reminisced about Octavio Ortiz, an energetic priest who was killed while directing a youth retreat in San Antonio de Abad on January 20th. A breeze blew through the slanted glass-louvered window, waving the flowered curtains as one man told of the priest's head being crushed. The retreat house had been demolished by tanks during the battle. The men spoke proudly of the church's heroic struggle, and of its courage in backing popular movements. They recalled the May 1, 1979 demonstrations and "actions" following the government beatings of labor leaders, including Facundo Guardo, a *campesino* leader, founder of the landowners' union, and leader of the BPR. Placido Erdozain remembers the day as ". . . a militant popular demonstration on May Day that involved the people's takeover of churches and embassies, and massacres by the military in the cathedral plaza and in the vicinity of the Venezuelan embassy. They fled up the steps of the cathedral as their blood trickled down. Forty-eight persons from the popular movement were dead. We were able to rescue three leaders from the clutches of the tyrants, but three others disappeared, and we had to assume they were dead."

If these forces of terror remained, how would the new government deal with them? The junta had promised to investigate murders, deaths and abductions, but would it investigate the death squads and their accomplices in the security forces? Would the new government allow peasant and labor groups to carry their message to the public? Would the church's commitment to social change be considered genuine? It seemed that no one could be trusted.

A much clearer reaction to the coup came from the leaders of the armed insurgency groups. To them, the takeover was a defeat, because the junta apparently was going to go along with the United States pressure for human rights. The coup represented new evidence that the government was essentially reactionary. "The Americans are playing games again, setting up puppets to deny us our triumph," was frequently heard around campfires of guerrilla unit bases. Young men, many of them survivors of government massacres and death squad violence, sat in small groups quietly talking as they smoked cheap cigarettes and rubbed grease on the clips of the German G3 automatic rifles or their old .45 pistol triggers. They wondered how the government would employ the 16,300 man army, navy, air force, national guard, national police, treasury and customs police, plus the thousands of death squad and private armed groups. What they wondered most was why they should no longer consider the new government the enemy.

In late 1979 the armed, insurgent left worked on strategic, tactical plans to obtain either a political or military victory.

The left reasoned that a political victory could come if Ungo and Roman Mayorga took an upper hand in the junta and then used that power to further the political transformation, getting rid of Majano, Gutierrez and a whole segment of the military. A military victory was not likely. However, there were rumors that better arms could be purchased internationally and then be transported from across the borders of Honduras, Nicaragua or Costa Rica. The leftists even talked about getting help from the socialist countries and other international revolutionary forces.

A military victory required better weapons than assorted pistols, shotguns, hunting rifles and a few good smuggled guns. Several leaders making the rounds of guerrilla groups promised their men, "We will have DKZ-57 antitank rocket launchers, AR-15 semiautomatics, UZI's, Galil's and more Claymore mines. Everyone here will have a 9mm pistol. We will be able to attack them with 50 caliber machine guns; we will have radios." Most revolutionary leaders correctly concluded that a military solution was more likely than a political one if they could continue to build and arm insurgent strength.

Apparently, there was little noticeable difference in the life of hundreds of thousands of Salvadorans in the days after the coup. Inside the government, rightists were making their strength known. Security forces continued to carry out their missions with impunity. To Majano and Gutierrez, it must have become clear that there really was no depth of support for the announced reforms.

By January 1980, most of the cabinet and all civilian members of the junta had resigned from the government. On January 8th, the Bloque Popular Revolucionario, the LP-28 and the FAPU issued an appeal for uprisings and a "peoples' war" against the government. In a three month old junta, it was difficult to determine whether or not El Salvador's political problems and the social attitudes could be changed. Were the moderates excessively hasty in their expectations? These groups might have been more successful pressing for moderation. Cooperation with the junta and a gradual easing out of extreme rightists might have worked better for the moderates. Or were the reactionary forces within the junta, who apparently threatened the moderates, still in control?

As to so many other questions about the situation in El Salvador, the answers are uncertain. On January 9, in an effort to reconcile at least part of the remaining civilian political forces, a new junta including two Christian democrats, lawyer José Antonio Morales Ehrlich and engineer Héctor Dada, was formed. Also, an Independent, Dr. Ramon Avalos Navarette, a heart surgeon, joined the ruling group. This junta was criticized by liberals in the Catholic church, by center and left-of-center political leaders, and by the guerrilla forces. In turn, the Salvadoran Communist Party and leftist groups formed "the Revolutionary Coordinating Committee for the Masses." The new junta was divided between conservative and moderate forces, especially in the military. Whatever good intentions there may have been — and there is little reason to doubt that reform-oriented efforts were being negotiated — excesses of rightists, especially retired Major Roberto D'Aubuisson's Broad National Front and the supporters of the recently abolished ORDEN, and the leftists, caused this moderate transition to flounder. Attempting to expropriate land and banks from private ownership brought reform technicians in the bureaucracy into direct conflict with El Salvador's leading power groups. Few of these gave the early reform efforts a chance. Leftists, however, immediately demonstrated their opposition to the junta by shooting Colonel Simon Tadeo Martell, Deputy Inspector General of the Armed Forces. They also seized government buildings, holding at least two cabinet members and hundreds of employees hostage. They then took over the national cathedral. The National Guard's Chief of

Investigations was gunned down, two major newspaper offices were bombed, and the U.S. Embassy was attacked by two hundred leftist demonstrators on October 30, 1979. The attackers were repelled by Marine guards and Salvadoran troops. Shortly thereafter, rightists surrounded the U.S. ambassador's home. As the left attempted to gain control, calls for peace fell on deaf ears. The Popular Revolutionary Bloc emerged as the most aggressive insurgent group, claiming responsibility for political shootings, bombings, kidnappings and the seizure of buildings. Most damaging of all was the internal fragmentation of the left. Just as the Revolutionary Bloc negotiated a truce with the junta, the leftist United Action Front announced an all out war against the government.

Leftists kidnapped South African Ambassador Gardner Dunn (who was executed a year later by the FPL while still in captivity), killed a prominent ex-mayor and blew up six planes at an airport. It is reported that two thousand leftists attacked ten thousand women marching against the violence. In the attack, buses were burned, three women died and dozens were injured. As usual, the plight of rural and small towns people went unreported. There was great fear and suffering in these areas, just as there was in the capital city.

One thing is clear from the events unfolding in El Salvador in 1979 — reconciliation, reform and peace were unacceptable by both the extreme right and the extreme left. In either case, politics was considered an "all-or-nothing" proposition. Attempts to gain absolute political control, instead of compromising with opposition groups, is characteristic of recent, polarized conditions in Latin America. Many incumbent regimes share this view, denying rights to opposition forces.

In the early months of the Gutierrez-Majano led junta a new start might have been made. However, the rightists were justifiably anxious about the friendly gestures the government made towards Cuba and Nicaragua, even though these gestures were at least partially an effort to accommodate socialist elements. Also, land redistribution and other reforms were distasteful to Salvadoran conservatives. The left believed that it could win. Moreover, leftists did not trust a government which had vast connections with existing institutions, particularly the military. It is difficult to second-guess the intentions of the junta, but it appears that it might have tried to restore stability and a measure of civil rights and push for economic and social reforms. In order to do this, however, moderates needed the cooperation of armed groups from both the left and right. Neither group was prepared to yield to an uncertain compromise.

Ambassador Devine's remark best presents the situation faced by the junta. Devine said that ". . . elections became something of a buzz word in El Salvador, and one's position on them was interpreted as showing whether that person was for or against reform. This was not generally understood in the United States and, particularly in Congress, where many members felt that elections are always good. As a result, well-intentioned spokesmen at home, by pushing for early elections in El Salvador, ran the unintended risk of identifying us with the anti-reforms sentiment of conservative groups. . . "

The fact that elections are so unrepresentative of the people only aids in perpetuating the violence and bitter struggle. It is little wonder that the junta failed. The pressures of groups within the country and by outsiders was too great. It could not survive.

9

The Carter/Reagan Policies: Reform, Repression or Revolution?

With the government weakened by the resignation of Christian Democrat Héctor Dada, and violence escalating, the junta declared a state of seige on March 6, 1980. It also issued a number of reform decrees, including the nationalization of banks. The state would now own 51 percent of each bank, with 29 percent of the shares sold to the public, and 20 percent sold to the bank's employees. No individual was permitted to own more than two percent of the shares. The new agrarian reform program, too, was set in motion with Decree 153 of 1980, of which a U.S. government report stated ". . . It can already be classed as among the most fundamental reforms ever to be undertaken."

A new U.S. ambassador, Robert E. White, arrived in San Salvador at this time. In his previous posts (notably Paraguay), White was known as an outspoken human rights advocate. The new American Ambassador stated that he would monitor and publicize human rights violations by the government. White's nomination was strongly opposed by Senator Jesse Helms, who objected to sending a liberal into a war-torn country. Helms said, "The nomination of Mr. White is like a torch tossed into a pool of oil." Helms argued that since 1962 the U.S. had ". . . constantly intervened in the internal affairs of El Salvador. . . " pushing it to the left. Helms concluded that by most conventional measures of social progress, El Salvador ". . . is one of the most enlightened countries in Latin America."

Of course, Salvadoran rightists also disliked White for his legendary feud with El Salvador's most conservative politician, Major Roberto d'Aubuisson. More interesting, however, are the references made by leftist revolutionary groups. Leftist journalist Mario Menendez interpreted the appointment of White as part of a policy that included ". . . the incorporation of several thousand North American mercenaries, Somalis, Saigonese, Guatemalans and Cuban counter-revolutionaries in the ranks of private armies at the service of the fourteen families and with the sharpening of repression in El Salvador."

Thus, while Ambassador White's appointment was heralded by U.S. human rights advocates and activists, Salvadoran revolutionaries took the opposite position, referring to the new American ambassador as ". . . the advisor to Paraguay's dictator Alfredo Stroessner and specialist in counter-insurgency war."

Salvador Cayetano Carpio, leader of the most powerful Marxist guerrilla organization, the Farabundo Marti Popular Liberation Forces, said White was ". . . nothing more and nothing less than the advisor to Stroessner's tyranny in Paraguay; that is to say, advisor to one of the most horrendous tyrannies suffered by any people in the American continent."

Carpio found it significant that White was sent to El

Salvador in the first months after the military coup. "Well then," Carpio said, "this advisor of assassins and hangmen, expert in counter-revolution, in massacres and oppression is the one the Department of State of the U.S. has chosen as the advisor of the Salvadoran military."

It is clear that the Salvadoran left wing never believed that the United States was truly committed to either political reform or improvement of civil rights.

Second in importance only to human rights was the U.S. imposed land reform program. By July 1980, 27 percent of the country's land had been included in the land reform program. Over half of all the land in the country was to be included upon the completion of Phase II. The law provided that most land holdings of over 100 hectares be redistributed. The army and about 800 agricultural sector technicians moved into the countryside to begin breaking up the holdings over 500 hectares. In addition to this agrarian reform process, Decree 207 — the "Land to the Tiller" law — was aimed at helping roughly 160,000 farm families working, but not owning, some 200,000 hectares of land. Incredibly, the reforms continued at a rapid pace through the early period of instability.

One dilemma of the reforms is that they were redistributive, taking property, assets and the concomitant power from families and individuals, then transferring these to other persons or the state. In this process corruption, fraud, embezzlement and outright thievery took a heavy toll. It was no secret that many government officials became wealthy by profiting from the reforms — not an unusual development even in the most democratic of Latin American countries.

Such reforms, of course, would scarcely have been tolerated by citizens of the United States. The breaking up of the largest farms and expropriation of banks would be unconstitutional in the United States. Even if legalized through legislation or decree, one could foresee bloody resistance by

American property owners. In an informal discussion, one group of U.S. farmers was given the following "land reform" scenario. "Your land will be given to landless sharecroppers, migrant workers, tenant farmers and young persons wanting to get into farming. You will be compensated with government bonds." The reaction of most of the farmers in this discussion was surprisingly violent. In El Salvador, however, the U.S. Agency for International Development is the main financier and technical supporter of such expropriation. One Salvadoran whose cotton farm was "reformed" and who now lives in the United States asked, "Why are U.S. farms getting bigger and bigger, and that's supposed to increase productivity, while in my country the same U.S. government is saying, 'Hey, you own too much land'? "

One AID report includes an interesting impressionistic evaluation of the reforms and U.S. policy. It states:

> The Salvadoran reality includes a damaged economy, grinding poverty, civil disorder, massive unemployment, violence and the threat of violence. It includes a private sector that is increasingly accepting reform, and is now willing to work; it, however, also lacks resources.
>
> The Salvadoran reality is now also characterized, however, by a new hope in the countryside—albeit mingled with fear and insecurity; by a

new work mystique among ISTA and MAG field staff, by tears in the eyes of old *colonos* as they witness the formal installation of their association's new *Junta Directiva;* by a fierce determiniation on the part of many *campesinos* to work to make a reform that is increasingly theirs a reality; and finally by a small, but growing group of noble Salvadorans who, even though they could fly to Miami or Costa Rica when their lives are threatened, continue to work fourteen hours a day, seven days a week to make El Salvador work again, to make their reform a reality, and to make their country a freer one and keep it that way.

It is for the latter reality, as well as the United States' own self-interest that El Salvador's agrarian reform merits AID's full support with appropriate funding instruments and levels to do the job. If others will not, or can not help, then we must do the job alone. If we do not, or allow our institutional inertia to get in the way, then El Salvador could become a major U.S. foreign policy disaster. We helped rebuild a war-torn Europe after World War II. Surely, we have the ability and capacity to make available levels of effective assistance to El Salvador today.

The possibility of massive reforms pushed by the United States, and supported by moderates and technocrats was interpreted differently by various groups. In my discussions with politicians, farm experts, and policy advisors, the reforms have been viewed as unprecedented and revolutionary. Many, in fact, call the Salvadoran government after March 1980 "The Socialist (or Communist) Junta." The left, reform-oriented groups and human rights' activists, on the other hand, generally dismiss the reforms as "window dressing" and refer to the government as "The Reactionary Right-Wing Junta." An intended immediate objective of the agrarian reform was to firmly establish the Salvadoran government's reputation as a "reform" junta whose goal has not been reached.

The left always rejected land reforms as a trick and as a joke. Schafik Jorge Handal, secretary general of El Salvador's Communist Party, recently said, "There is no possibility for a reformist way out of the national crisis." He states that El Salvador's elite has deep and ancient agrarian roots and thus has developed a "Prussian mentality; opposing definitively any profound reform or social transformation."

Tomás Guerra quotes Father Ignacio Ellacuria, rector of the Catholic University in El Salvador, as saying that the reform of the junta, especially land reform is ". . . a purely North American project, the goal of which is to annul popular resistance." Guerra concludes that no one in El Salvador has bought the sincerity or effectiveness of land reform. He lumps it together with the expansion of U.S. counter-insurgency assistance to the Salvadoran government. "The reforms are intended to deceive the people, calm them down with promises; to then re-establish the previous, inhuman state of affairs."

Some other serious questions about the land reform were soon raised by outside organizations such as OXFAM America.

In the 1980-81 audit of the land reform, James C. Stephens, Jr. summarizes the findings of the report as follows:

"1) Over 60 percent of El Salvador's rural population are not potential beneficiaries for the current land reform. 2) The current land reform program excludes the poorest and largest section of the rural population— landless rural laborers. 3) The land reform is a "top-down" model solution imposed on the government and people of El Salvador by agencies and advisors under contract to the U.S. government. 4) The peasantry, church, academics, and agrarian experts of El Salvador have been excluded from the design, planning and implementation of the current agrarian reform. 5) The entire program suffers from a critical lack of planning and development implementing regulations. 6) The land reform program has been implemented in the context of increasing and unrelenting levels of violence against the rural population.

Another writer, Martin Diskin of M.I.T., concludes that the land reform, conceived in haste, is too modest to make any difference to the life of most poor, rural Salvadorans. He further argues that the implementation of the program has been so slow that there have been changes made which weaken or even cancel what progress there was. Diskin concludes that " . . . whatever possibilities this approach might have had, are effectively neutralized."

U.S. Ambassador White stepped into an almost impossibly complex situation. We cannot judge if he indeed felt that a non-Communist reform process had any chance of success. He spoke about the United States supporting the " . . . voice of reason and reform: We believe the creative center must be expanded at the expense of the sterile extremes."

Where ambassador White felt such a coalition could be found, and how he felt the extremes at both ends could be defeated, is not clear. I have asked him that question, and he still talks about the possibility of a political solution— getting the extremists to negotiate a peace and eventually providing for fair elections.

During White's short tenure in San Salvador, many of the moderate-leftist politicians were abducted, murdered, or fled to exile; four U.S. churchwomen were murdered; and two U.S. land reform consultants and the director of the land reform institue, José Rudolfo Viera, were gunned down at the Sheraton Hotel. Archbishop Romero was cut down by a right-wing hired gun; tons of arms were funneled to the insurgents; peasants, villagers, workers, and clergy were slaughtered; the U.S. embassy was fired on and attacked with rockets; businesses and factories were closed; and, capital fled the country.

As conditions continued to deteriorate, the junta was reorganized. When Christian Democrat José Napoleón Duarte, a civil engineer educated at Notre Dame, was named President in December 1980, it was hoped that moderates would support the government. However, many have argued that Duarte was merely a figurehead. I would maintain that any evaluation of Duarte, between his ascent to the presidency and early 1982, must be based on the outcome of events. Even Duarte admitted that he was not completely in control. In March 1981, he said to a *Newsweek* writer, Beth Nissen, "How can I control every soldier? How can I stop the fourteen-year-old who has been trained to hate and to kill what he hates? "

Leaders of the revolutionary PRN-FARN dismissed Duarte as a rightist Christian Democrat who wanted to strengthen ties with the fourteen families and their protectors— the military. "Slaughter and reform" is what one revolutionary called Duarte's 1981 program. Guerra suggested that the Duarte government was not made up of diverse ideological groups, but rather a single, North American inspired reformist clique centered in the private Central American University (UCA) in San Salvador.

Since Duarte supposedly represented a "middle ground," it is important to stress that Salvadoran revolutionaries have rejected this so-called "third historical alternative." "This crisis" says Guerra, "cannot be resolved along this road as some elements of imperialism, the bourgeoisie and middle class argue. Efforts to save reformist projects, now frantically supported by the U.S. government, are condemned to failure."

Any government in El Salvador faces almost insurmountable problems, even under the best of political and economic conditions. We are dealing with a pre-industrial society, a reality frequently overlooked by experts from the highly industrialized world. There is no effective government organization, no economic stability, no real middle class, little education and no solid industrial or economic base. There is little individual freedom, and even less security. And yet, any government that assumes power in El Salvador is expected to deal effectively with these problems. Neither the extreme right nor the extreme left will accept anything but total success.

El Salvador, at least since 1977, has been faced with certain "realities" of global politics. These critical issues are crucial in understanding domestic events there.

First, El Salvador was one of President Carter's early test cases for human rights. This focuses a significant amount of attention on a difficult situation. Inevitably, the pressures for economic "reform," which were brought to bear on the Salvadoran government since Carter's inauguration, were going to vastly escalate violence and unrest. As the unrest grew, reactionary forces resisted and pushed, and centrist groups wobbled and waffled. Everyone seemed surprised at the rising brutality and growing instability. In retrospect, the Carter Administration may have misinterpreted the range and spectrum of options which could realistically work in this embattled nation. A centrist reform government completely lacking in a political power base, apparently clumsy at mobilizing people and marshalling broad popular support, was probably the least stable regime on which to place one's faith. Centrism and reform have largely been a figment of the American imagination. What few genuinely moderate forces existed in the country were buffeted between conservatives in the military; landowners and others who were losing power and assets in the reform programs; right-wing death squads; liberal reformers; and extreme left terrorist hit squads and revolutionary guerrillas. The center's ability to fight back never materialized.

The various reforms, announced and initiated by the junta and pushed back by the United States, had two immediate consequences: One, they completely wiped out what remaining support or even acquiescence the government might have had from the right. Two, they triggered a violent reaction by the left, which was militantly against such reforms. It is instructive that, soon after the junta made known its plans, a leftist demonstration by the LP-28 (the street organization controlled by the guerrilla group ERP) attacked the U.S. Embassy. About noon on October 30, 1979, over 200 people marched from the university to the embassy. The huge banners they were carrying were really camouflage for five long ladders. The demonstrators rushed the embassy, whipping out Uzi submachine guns, rifles, and pistols, and putting the U.S. Mission under armed seige. The leftists were eventually repelled by the Marine guards.

On January 22, 1980, leftist gunmen bombed and attacked the private residence of the U.S. ambassador. At the same time, guerrillas kidnapped, harassed and threatened lives of U.S. Peace Corps volunteers. By March 1980, all the volunteers were effectively removed from El Salvador. During Ambassador White's tenure, rightist demonstrators— also opposed to reformism— surrounded his residence and he had to be rescued by the Embassy Marine Guard detachment.

Second, the El Salvador crisis began to unravel at the tail end of a frustrating period in American foreign policy. South Vietnam fell into communist hands; Laos collapsed; Cambodia descended into the madness of Pol Pot and then was, for all practical purposes, annexed by Vietnam; Ethiopia became a Soviet ally; Angola was liberated by Marxist nationalists; Iran got rid of a Shah and gained 53 American hostages; Afghanistan was occupied by Russian troops; and U.S. embassies in Libya and Pakistan were burned. Closer to home, Fidel Castro unleashed a barrage of difficult challenges — over 100,000 new Cuban refugees were sent into Florida. Castro embraced Nicaraguans on the anniversary of Somoza's fall, and thousands of Cuban teachers, as well as military advisors, flew to Managua. Castro became a patron and model for Jamaica, Guyana and Grenada. Soviet troops were restless and snooped around the Polish border. The United States' response to these indignities and international challenges was always somewhat ambiguous. I believe the Carter Administration was not aware how insulted and furious many people on "Main Street U.S.A." were, especially at the indignities aimed directly at the United States, American diplomats and the U.S. flag.

Third, President Jimmy Carter was opposed by Reagan in the 1980 election. A strong conservative challenge was mounted against moderate and liberal congressmen and senators. As the U.S. campaign began to unfold, the contending forces in Central America, particularly in El Salvador, were placing their own bets. The left began to press harder. The right also stepped up its resolve. If Reagan won, it was felt that the emphasis of U.S. policy would be shifted toward a harder, conservative, more anti-Communist, more military line. Thus, from the moment the Republican convention picked its national ticket in Detroit, the situation in El Salvador was colored by the possible ideological shift in the United States. Neither the right nor the left were about to cooperate with the ruling junta.

Fourth, when Ronald Reagan won the 1980 presidential election, the Republican victory appeared to give the new U.S. government a mandate to get tough with the Soviet Union, with Cuba and with their clients, surrogates, and potential allies. El Salvador was designated by Secretary of State Alexander Haig as the natural place to draw the line. El Salvador would also be the place where the success and purposes of U.S. technical, military, and economic assistance would be tested. Reagan transition team members and unofficial Reagan supporters traveled to Central America declaring that Reagan favored a rightist solution. In these hectic weeks, several corpses in El Salvador were found with signs around their necks saying, "Now that Reagan is President, we will kill all communists."

Fifth, Central America has a peculiar familiarity about it. To some, it looks a great deal like Southeast Asia twenty years ago. Domino theorists in Washington began musing that Nicaragua is the area's North Vietnam; El Salvador is the functional equivalent of South Vietnam; Honduras is Cambodia and Laos; and, Guatemala is Thailand. For many, names like Cusnahuat, Nejapa, Uluazapa, Cacopera and Metapán (all in El Salvador), sound much like provincial villages in Southeast Asia. In late March, 1981, Vietnam as an analogy even entered reporters' questions of President Reagan, National Security Advisor Richard Allen and Secretary of State Alexander Haig. Congressmen and the media also began to talk about "another Vietnam." Even Salvadoran revolutionaries believed they were the cutting edge of a battle against imperialism in all Central America.

Sixth, we should add to the geographic analogy a premise

shared by some in the new administration— the United States must overcome its "gun shyness" about using military force. Overcoming the post-Vietnam isolationism is said to be a necessary catharsis to bring maturity and self-confidence back to the U.S. political body. Several goals in our future foreign affairs, it is argued, can be more successfully realized if we put "Vietnam behind us." Among these goals, checking Cuban "adventures" and support for various ultra conservative groups is quite important. Ronald Reagan, it must be remembered, early on raised the possibility of a blockade as one way to stem Cuban subversion. Giving the Russians pause about foreign adventures is another objective which "getting tough" can supposedly help accomplish. Reverses in American global objectives during the decade of the 1970s are attributed by some in Washington as a by-product of the notion that the Vietnam experience had effectively neutralized the use and support of force by the United States. Talking tough, as Secretary of State Haig did during his first days in office, was one phase of this post-Vietnam posturing. Vast increases in military spending is another. Taking some kind of action in Central America is a third stage in the process. Giving military aid and selling arms to Chile, Argentina and others were contemplated.

Seventh, the Carter Administration was seen by conservatives as the best proof that emphasis on human rights is not a good cornerstone for U.S. foreign policy. Several developments contributed to this erosion of confidence in human rights' programs. Most tragic and dramatic, of course, were the events in Iran following the fall of the Shah. It would be hard to argue that the violence, strife, reversal of women's rights, liberal use of capital punishment, repression of regional, ethnic and religious minorities, and the arbitrary arrests (not only of foreign citizens and diplomats but also of Iranians) are an improvement in human rights.

The overthrow of Anastasio Somoza in Nicaragua was also supported and eventually encouraged by the Carter Administration. Doubts about the new regime in Managua caused the U.S. Congress, from the very beginning, to delay a vitally necessary assistance package. The Nicaraguans then took aid from wherever it came, largely from East Germany, Cuba, and other socialist countries. With political pluralism rapidly eroding in Nicaragua and with its practical and symbolic role as the centerpiece of Central American liberation movements established, conservatives again point to the folly of Carter's human rights' policy. It is interesting to add that all Latin American political leaders and analysts with whom I've spoken consider Nicaragua now to be simply another Cuba.

Eighth, U.S. relations with Chile, Brazil, Uruguay, Guatemala and Argentina (until the Falkland War), all of which have serious human rights' problems, have been somewhat normalized by the Reagan government.

It appears that confusion over human rights in the 1980s is a reality. Nonetheless, in September 1981, the U.S. Senate attached provisions to the foreign aid bill which would require a bi-annual review of human rights conditions in El Salvador before U.S. assistance is continued. U.S. aid to that country would be contingent on "progress" in several areas. Salvadoran President Duarte spent the latter part of September 1981 in the United States lobbying for continued U.S. support. During his visit, Duarte was subjected to extensive protests and accusations as to his government's complicity in human rights' violations.

The irony of human rights' debates is that such great disagreement exists over several elements. First, how does one assure progress in human rights' conditions as one regime crumbles and another emerges? Second, is anti-regime violence and terrorism considered a human rights' violation? Third, what is the best method of forcing improvements in conditions? Do grain embargoes, Olympic boycotts, cutting of foreign aid, publicly castigating governments, reducing the levels of diplomatic interaction, restricting trade and tourism, and cautioning U.S. investors accomplish the goal of forcing better conditions? Should other measures (including covert action and perhaps arming and recognizing opponents of guilty regimes) be considered?   Or is the Reagan Administration on the right track with its idea of behind-the-scenes pressure to change oppressive government civil rights' policies? Are revolutionary activities which aim at bringing change and justice to a people, but which require force and violence, justifiable if people's human rights are violated? For example, during the Russian, Chinese, Mexican, Cuban and other revolutions, due process and other measures of human rights were abrogated. If the government of Nicaragua finds it necessary to arrest, imprison or execute enemies of the state in order to protect the government against counter-revolutionaries, is this a human rights' violation or is it simply the legitimate right of the state to defend itself?

Summary executions, torture, arbitrary arrest, and "disappearances" are never justified from an objective and humanistic point of view. However, they are often the concomitant of political and social movements or events. Moreover, one person's human rights' violation appears to be another's legitimate war, just as one's terrorist is another's freedom fighter. Moreover, monitoring and intervening on behalf of human rights requires precise intervention in the affairs of other states. The judgement on how much and what sort of intervention is justified in defense of human rights remains unclear. The options range from diplomatically discouraging violations to supporting the overthrow of oppressive governments. Understandably, many persons are confused by the practical options in the pursuit of human rights. Human rights is a very political matter.

Yet these judgements and external constraints are the "reality" within which the Salvadoran government of José Napoleón Duarte had to operate.   Foreign journalists in droves reported from San Salvador, from little villages, and even from guerrilla base camps. Congressmen and senators traveled for a "first-hand look" at the situation. Bianca Jagger commiserated with Salvadoran refugees in Honduras. T.V. personality Ed Asner spoke out and declared his support for the guerrillas. All these events were on the morning news and in all American newspapers. U.S. human rights' groups were constantly looking over the government's shoulder. The American people could not allow any more U.S. advisors, technical military instructors, or aid to be flown to El Salvador. And even when a U.S. military advisor carried a M-16 rifle for personal protection, and it was filmed by Cable News Network, a furor arose which reverberated right into the Oval Office of the White House. Demonstrators in Europe and Latin America chimed in their opposition to the Duarte government. When four Dutch newsmen were killed in a remote area of El Salvador in March 1982, the Dutch government hinted that it would recognize the guerrillas as the legitimate representatives of the Salvadoran people. What must be clear to the Salvadoran regime is that these are the given conditions; that cannot be changed. So the government must find a way to perform within these standards or eventually be abandoned as an unworkable regime.

In sum, the juntas were, from the very start, doomed because, as Ambassador White has stated, the United States was anxious to build a "contrived" center. Most people agree that there really was no political center. Moreover, the strategy of change from the top down, of authoritarian solutions imposed from the central government, was probably a big mistake.

People did not feel a part of the problem-solving process and, therefore, the reforms were seen as coming from the outside. Also, there seems to have been a mistaken notion, especially among U.S. development agencies, that the initiation of reforms automatically and concurrently generates political support for the regime. Since the land reforms envisioned would eventually be affecting most farms in the country, the first effect was to drive all landowners from supporting the junta. Another result of the land reform was the false assumption that newly propertied peasants would become visible, articulate, and passionate supporters of the center, and thus help build this base on which future stability might rest. On close inspection, it becomes clear that there was never an effort made to mobilize supporters and beneficiaries of these reforms. Without conscious political mobilization, such support could never materialize, and indeed, did not.

Attacked by right and left, not fully in control of its own security forces, having cut itself off from the last vestige of support of the conservative center, the junta lurched from crisis to crisis. Each week that passed exacerbated the Duarte government's problems with human rights. Soon, demonstrators in European cities were singing the praises of the Salvadoran revolutionary left. American technical advisors, helicopters and military aid only heightened the concern in the United States over the possible "new Vietnam" in Central America. A *Washington Post* poll showed that over half of the American public would support draft resisters against the possibility of being forced to fight in El Salvador. While the Reagan Administration insisted that Duarte was the best hope of stemming the fall of yet another Central American "domino" (Nicaragua being written off as already down), President Duarte soon found his base of support limited to a small segment of the U.S. government and a portion of the armed forces of El Salvador.

There are those who argue that even the U.S. government never really believed in early 1982 that the center could maintain its power. President Reagan and Secretary of State Alexander Haig really hoped for a tough rightist solution. Liberals in the United States hoped Duarte would leave gracefully, making room for the only people who, in their eyes, could give the Salvadoran people a better life; namely, the coalition of leftist anti-government forces. Whether this left-right perspective actually prevailed underneath all the rhetoric of "moderate forces" and "progressive center" is not clear. However, it seems reasonable.

The sad truth is that while the United States had been able to transfer millions of dollars in economic and military assistance to the Duarte government, it apparently had absolutely no capability of also providing "political development aid." The Agency for International Development was not prepared to fund projects or consulting work in which a government such as the "center" junta of El Salvador could learn some badly-needed skills — skills required to build a base of support among those sectors which are the supposed beneficiaries of the reform. Looking back at late 1979, 1980, 1981 and early 1982, one must conclude that it was essentially the United States-backed reforms which helped further destabilize El Salvador. Such contested and controversial reforms carried out by a regime with no political base and few political skills will irritate and even trigger violence rather than stimulate "hope" and "support." So long as the U.S. government continues to shy away from providing a whole new level of technical assistance — that which generates political mobilization and peaceful channels of participation alongside the technical reform — these efforts, such as land reform, should be avoided. The elections of March 1982, in the midst of carnage and through which the right became stronger, are simply another indicator of the inadequate political assistance flowing from Washington.

Reforms in a setting of violence, brutality and internecine conflict do not appear to be very realistic. This should become clear when we look more carefully at the levels of violence affecting El Salvador and at the profound ideological rifts which have plunged even such stable institutions as the Catholic Church into the abyss of Salvadoran politics.

10

Death and Violence

Francisco Baltazar Campos Mendoza will never forget the bus ride he took on October 25, 1978. He was arrested at La Union and taken to National Guard headquarters in San Miguel where he was interrogated and beaten. For twenty-eight days Campos was shuffled between several security barracks. Campos was forced to confess that he belonged to the revolutionary FPL organization. His captors also tried to extract information on subversives. "We have ways of making you talk," they threatened. One day he was dragged into an interrogation room and his head was covered with a plastic bag. His captors slowly tightened a cord around

132

the bottom of the bag at his neck. They made Campos stand, then threw powerful punches to his stomach. When he gasped for air, the plastic bag compressed against his face. After each blow he would gasp, the bag smothering his nostrils and her-mertically sealing his mouth. He struggled frantically for air—twitching, asphyxiating — finally losing consciousness and col-lapsing in a heap on the floor.

Not satisfied with Campos' answers, his captor resorted to other forms of torture. His testicles were forced into a bag of ice and freezing water. When they were thoroughly chilled, the bag was repeatedly jerked downward. Needle-like pain shot from his scrotum throughout his whole body. On another oc-casion, Campos suffered great fear and pain when a thick metal rod was inserted into his rectum. Electric shocks were applied to his body.

One morning, Campos was awakened, dragged out of his cell and taken to a lake. He was told that he would be drowned if he did not talk. His captors then held the barrel of a pistol to his face, firing a shot which barely grazed his skull. They quickly turned him, held the pistol to his right temple and fired. Campos had mentally prepared to die. But the gun was empty. For Campos, the mock execution was a classic in mental tor-ture.

Campos was always kept nude and his hands and feet were handcuffed to an iron bed each night. He was unable to scratch, drink, eat or urinate. His captors told him that he would be set free, but added, "First we need to give you an in-jection of vitamins." After the liquid shot into his vein, Cam-pos felt dizzy and helpless, his muscle control gone. He was stuffed into a car and driven to a place near Ciudad Arce, where he was dumped. Barely conscious, he realized that sev-eral charges of dynamite were beside his head and the fuses were lit. Campos rolled sideways into the safety of a small ditch just before the dynamite exploded.

Campos' ordeal ended on November 28 when he asked

the Mexican Embassy for asylum. But for most Salvadorans, the violence continues. Violence and death are experienced so frequently that they have become an integral part of Salvadoran culture.

The acceptance of death by Mexicans has been commented upon by Jacques Soustelle, who speaks of the casual acceptance of death when he says, "Death and life are no more than two sides of the same reality; from the earliest times the potters of Tlatilco made a double face, one-half alive and the other skull-like."

The cult of death appears in the myths and folklore of all Central American cultures — blood, death and sacrifice being integral parts of their ritual religious ceremony. The Spanish tradition that embodied Arabic, Germanic, Semitic and other cultures also celebrated death. Spaniards display ". . . a certain indifference to pain, almost a love of it, " comments Ellis. Spanish martyrs continued to sing when they were being nailed to the cross and Spanish mothers would kill their children rather than let them become slaves.

Barbara Brodman believes that the cult of death was newly imprinted on Mexican and Central American culture when the Iberian and native cultures clashed and melded. Another researcher argues that after the Spanish conquest, Mexicans were subjected to more violence than any other people. Death was so pervasive that facing it became a singularly important test of virility. The popular saying, "Tell me how you'll die and I'll tell you who you are," shows the cockiness with which many Latin Americans view death.

This acceptance of death appears peculiar to the outsider. Tourists are surprised to see skeletons decorating Latin American discos. Brodman expresses surprise at the "exceedingly sanguinary" statuary. She is also struck by the "conspicuous presence of skulls, skeletons, mummies and other death objects of one material or another in virtually every household, and by the presence of these same objects as part of the decorations applied by bus drivers to the front of their vehicles."

But the most explicit evidence of the cult of the dead is the Day of the Dead, celebrated on November 2nd. On this day, it is believed that the dead may visit the earth. Skull-shaped candies and coffins are eaten, while funeral processions are filled with paper figures of dead loved ones and relatives.

Brodman traces the cult of death through the writings of six Mexican authors. One of these writers, Juan Rulfo, tells of the impact that life in the state of Jalisco had on his writing. "The landscape . . . is decrepit. The living are surrounded by the dead . . . most people have migrated. Those who have stayed are there to keep the dead company."

Rulfo's view has been preserved in Mexican and Central American folklore. Supposedly, before a man leaves his village, his ancestors mentally tie him to the village, making him dig up their bones and carry them with him as he moves to a new life. Rulfo said, " . . . everyone died at the age of thirty-three." Rulfo's father and several of his uncles were murdered.

Murder and violence ultimately exist for their own sake. In the writing of many authors, the murderers are revolutionaries who have lost their original purpose. Politics, death and literature intertwine in the short stories Brodman cites, substantiating her hypothesis that the cult of death is a significant element of the modern Latin American psyche. This does not imply that Latin Americans, particularly Salvadorans, like death or violence. However, traditional Latin American society did view life as a transitional period — real happiness occurring only after one died and went to heaven. For this reason, infant deaths were considered a special blessing. Pastoral letters counselled parishioners to be patient, to suffer on this earth and reap one's happiness in the hereafter.

Death has always been near in El Salvador. Poor Salvadorans lack clean water, medical care, proper nutrition and hygiene. But it is the violence that draws attention to this situation. Other authoritarian governments and dictatorships have ruled ruthlessly, but have gone uncriticized because their violent acts were kept secret. In El Salvador, however, government violence is reported daily and graphically.

Violence committed against peasants and lower classes has probably always existed in El Salvador. The system of justice is unfair, and the poor are discouraged from appealing through higher courts because of legal fees. Judges are biased toward the ruling class and the patron-client relations heavily influence almost all adjudication proceedings. Interestingly, all government efforts to end this unfair practice have themselves been met with more violence. In a sense, neither the government nor the landowners can be said to have started this violence. Rather, they seem to have been drawn into it by each other.

Both used torture, rape, beatings and death threats as levers of political control. The most common forms of violence were small arms, bombs, arson, electrocution, strangulation, and cutting with knives or machetes. As well, ritual mutilation, especially decapitation, the disfigurement of genitalia, and male castration occurred frequently. In this respect, El Salvador resembles *La Violencia* in Colombia.

El Salvador's death and injury rate climbed to over 36,000 people by 1982. Salvadoran refugees were counted as victims. Those who fled the country were also considered victims. Such statistics are incidental to the El Salvador situation, which is primarily a result of a political way. However, understanding the various types of violence makes the situation clearer.

One type of violence, the revolutionary and counter-insurgency operations, pits government troops against guerrillas. The purpose of these operations is to win ground, control the populace, and eventually to win the war. When guerrillas clashed with troops, many died intentionally and accidentally. Most of the troops and guerrillas were inexperienced youngsters who had a tendency to shoot indiscriminately. The enemy was everywhere and could be anyone. This type of violence paralyzed the economy; its practitioners blew up electrical power grids and bridges, destroyed crops and bombed buildings.

Terrorism is a more widespread type of violence used by both left and right-wing extremists. The existence of terrorism on one side is given as justification for its use by the other side. Terrorism is also a tactic for killing the trained personnel of the opposition, and for forcing an adversary into submission. The left-wing often uses terrorism to force excesses on incumbent governments as a means of eroding their public support. In a turbulent situation such as El Salvador's, a death threat from the left or right is enough to make people flee.

Terrorism was used in the 1960s by leftist groups in Venezuela. The leftists hoped to sway public opinion toward their cause by drawing the military out against the civilian government. They also weakened the government's legitimacy by frightening people away from the polls.

Terrorism in the Soviet Union is legendary, and perhaps the best model of this type of violence. The Tzars had secret police, variously called the Oprichina, the Preobrazhensky office, and the Okhrana. The NKVD, which eventually became the KGB, was set up by Stalin in 1918 in order to arrest and punish suspected counter-revolutionaries. Stalin's infamous secret police arrested peasants who resisted land collectivization.

Lyman Holder analyzes the evolution of terrorism in Russian politics up to 1918 in his article, "They Shoot People, Don't They? A Look at Soviet Terrorist Mentality." Holder argues that the Russians inherited their ruthlessness, cruelty and disregard for human life from the ancient Tartars. He states that "Terrorism has been used for almost five centuries." For example, in the 1880s, General Strelnikov, " . . . a prosecutor active in the military courts of southern Russia during the 1880s, pioneered the concept of preemptive arrest of those thought likely to commit crimes of which they were actually innocent. Strelnikov practiced mass searches and arrests . . . seizing persons entirely unconnected with revolutionary activity . . . He felt it better to seize the innocents than to let one guilty person escape."

Tzar Ivan IV, "Ivan the Terrible" ultimately fell because he was not ruthless enough. Stalin felt that the Tzar spent too much time praying. He should have been terrorizing all potential opposition.

Stalin's view of terrorism as a tool for preserving the power of the state still exists in El Salvador. The Salvadoran revolutionaries, like the Bolsheviks, use terrorism to destabilize the government, then use it again to strengthen their power.

Terrorism is common throughout Latin America, and has been employed for many decades. Scholar-historian Dana Munro described the rule of Guatemalan strong man, Manuel Cabrera, in terms that fit El Salvador.

> The administration firmly maintains its authority by means of a large standing army and police force, and promptly and mercilessly checks the slightest manifestation of popular dissatisfaction. An elaborate secret service attempts, with a large measure of success, to inform itself fully of everything which occurs in the Republic. Supposed enemies of the party in power are closely watched, through their neighbors, their servants, and even through the members of their own families. . . It is dangerous to express an opinion on political matters even in private conversations. . .
> Persons who fall under suspicion are imprisoned or restricted in their liberty, or even mysteriously disappear."

Salvadoran revolutionary groups have used terrorism to frighten away foreign capital and business, to encourage flight of money from the nation's economy, to cast an aura of fear over soldiers and security troops, to persuade villagers into supporting the revolution, and to encourage defection from the government's armed forces.

According to James Berry, the terrorist justifies his actions by arguing that "society is sick and cannot be cured by half-measures of reform. The state is violent and can be overcome only by violence, and the truth of the terrorist cause justifies any action that supports it." Berry notes that the Algerian FLN used terrorism to further its struggle for national liberation against the French. ". . . the FLN purpose in planting bombs on public buses was not, as the French thought, to blow up the buses, but to lure authorities into reacting by arresting all the non-Europeans in the area as suspects, thus alienating the population. By failing to understand the strategy of terrorism the French were unable to perceive that it was not the FLN actions but rather the French countermove that in the end would determine the success or failure of the FLN cause."

National armies experience great problems in dealing effectively with prolonged terrorist violence. Police, intelligence services and para-military forces are often even less capable. The secret police has been used for decades as an instrument of political control by the government, therefore they have no long-term perspective on security, making them little more than "hired guns" of the ruling politicians. Of course, the average citizen is the least prepared to cope with terrorist brutality.

A third type of violence is the crime of opportunity, which accompanies all unstable situations. Just as looting inevitably follows natural disasters; theft, kidnapping and hold-ups have followed political chaos in El Salvador. Personal and impulsive crimes are easily committed when large quantities of guns are accessible, and law enforcement is almost non-existent. For example, Lil Milagro Ramirez revealed that her captors gang-raped and sexually abused her repeatedly.

Many societies use violence as a tool of justice. Chain gangs, public beatings, solitary confinement, stocks, and capital punishment are common forms of official violence. In traditional societies, personal vendettas are accepted as justice.

Feuding and crimes of passion are often personally vindicated. In many Latin American countries, it is not a punishable crime for an outraged husband to kill his wife and her lover.

A more sadistic type of violence is pathological violence. Thrill killings, mass murders and bizarre tortures have pathological roots, and commonly occur in situations such as El Salvador.

The reasons for violence are numerous, but in El Salvador, the evidence indicates that most of the killings are politically motivated. Terrorism there includes revolutionary and counter-insurgency killings. Ten years ago in Argentina, Uruguay and Chile, revolutionaries were struggling against government troops. Arrests and disappearances, kidnappings, bombings, and torture were successfully used by the Uruguayan government to crush the Tupamaros. The Argentine security forces defeated the Montoneros, though not without killing thousands of innocent people. The Chileans purged their government of Marxists, Allende supporters and everyone else opposed to the Pinochet government. Argentina, Uruguay and Chile have strongly influenced Latin American countries, including El Salvador. Salvadoran revolutionaries also have their models for using violence as a tool of revolution.

The Argentine-born Cuban revolutionary, Ché Guevara, outlined the relationship between violence and revolution. Jay Mallin writes that Ché Guevara "advocated the use of terror on the model of Giap. He saw terror not only as a means of intimidating civilians to support and help the guerrilla forces, but also as a means of forcing increasingly harsh and indiscriminate counter-measures on the part of government forces."

Guevara himself noted that "revolution was a long, difficult and cruel struggle. What do the dangers or the sacrifices of a man, or of a nation, matter when the destiny of humanity is at stake? "

Another revolutionary, Brazilian Carlos Marighela, identified the foundations of revolutionary violence and terrorism as deterrents against government opposition. Both factors are at work in El Salvador.

In 1981, the leftist forces claimed responsibility for 6,000 casualties in one year. The Salvadoran army estimated casualty rates as high as 20 percent. Government forces were the culprits in the bulk of civilian injuries and deaths.

The annual human rights report to the U.S. Congress explained the historical background of Salvadoran politics: "Killings and terrorist acts are the work of both leftist 'Democratic Front' forces who often claim responsibility for them, and of rightist elements with whom some members of the official security organizations are associated."

The report also indicated that summary executions were common. Both the government and the guerrillas went into villages carrying lists of suspected opponents, executing those named on the lists.

A further feature of political violence is the "join us or die" tactic, used to intimidate people and to trigger violence. Lists of victims published by the human rights' organizations clearly show that groups such as labor organizations, peasant leagues and clergy were targets of violence. These groups were often created outside the traditional structures of authority. In the case of some government-sponsored farmer groups, the violence was directed at these people by both the right and the left forces. The remaining reform-oriented segments of Salvadoran government were being attacked by the right and the left.

The Colombian violence of 1948-1962 is instructive. Peasant guerrillas fought against other peasants, and leftist officers fought against soldiers, landowners and peasants. Security forces contributed heavily to the violence, many times killing entire families. Victims were decapitated and scalped. They were also subjected to the *corte de chaleco* and *de franela*, in which three sides of a rectangle were cut on the chest and the skin ripped up. The practice of *no dejar ni una semilla* (not leaving even a seed) led to infanticide, male castration, mass rape-murder and tearing the fetuses from pregnant women.

The causes of rampant violence among peasants has not been well analyzed. However, in the Colombian case, "social disorganization, mental illness, aborted social revolution, revenge, political terrorism, natural cruelty, banditry, ethno-regional hatreds, clan wars, class wars, socio-economic repression, unfulfilled and perversely deflected sexuality, peasant justice and breakdown of governmental authority" have all been cited as reasons. The case of El Salvador is frustrating in regard to violence, because very little has been learned from other case studies that can be applied to its situation.

Americans began to show a serious interest in the violence in El Salvador only after four American church women, Archbishop Romero and two U.S. land reform advisors were killed. For Salvadoran peasants, death and violence have been predictable companions for many generations. It must be left to others to analyze the reasons why there appears to be a prominent place for death, a "cult of death" as it has been called by many scholars, in Latin American culture. Death and violence have coursed their way through the political history of these systems and deeply affected their social customs, including their political culture. Violence is, in fact, a more common political tool than elections.

Revolutionary groups, particularly Marxists, argue that the inequitable colonial and neo-colonial social structure of capitalism is the root cause of exploitation, repression and terrorism, imposed by landowners and other elite elements. The revolutionaries believe these views have been intentionally applied to preserve the skewed social order. However revolutionary groups of the left have never rejected the use of violence as a tactical instrument. Strategically applied, violence can achieve a number of goals; intimidating people into supporting revolutionary groups or deterring them from reporting to the authorities. Carefully targeted acts of violence can also provoke the power structure into excesses; or can ultimately lead to a political and military victory, and outright control of the government.

Conservative groups and right-wing governments, as well, have resorted to violence. Often a turbulent nineteenth century history filled with civil wars and invasions has made the use of violence a dominant political technique. This has been the case in El Salvador. Thus, in the latter 20th century there is still a tendency to view harsh measures as the best way to punish and deter those who might conspire against, or even criticize, the government. Therefore, wealthy, powerful groups, who stand to lose a great deal if progressive reforms are pushed through and who will lose everything if a Marxist regime comes to power, are lashing back at the reformists and at the revolutionaries. Terrorism, both revolutionary and counter-revolutionary, is clearly the number one cause of death in El Salvador.

Obviously, the revolutionaries and the threatened elite are both involved in an all-out struggle for victory. Each is the deadly enemy of the other. Marxist and non-Marxist revolutionaries rightly blame the old elite for the human misery and underdevelopment. The elite group accuses the revolutionaries of being "Godless communists who will ultimately enslave the people."

The ferocity with which the landowners and others fight can be understood if one imagines a group coming to power in the U.S., who expropriate land, homes, and possessions and who punish middle and upper-class citizens for their complicity in past "crimes against the people." These are not abstract examples, but are politics personalized to the highest degree.

The Salvadoran war of terror reveals many stories of human degradation. Reynaldo Cruz Menjivar from Nueve Concepcion has told a sordid tale of such degradation. He was arrested by treasury police and subjected to hunger, beatings, and every conceivable abuse. It is the story of societal collapse, and of the worst instincts in men.

"During the first six days of captivity," Menjivar wrote

"I got nothing to eat nor anything to drink. I was tormented, desperate and thirsty after losing so much blood in the brutal interrogations. My handcuffs were exceedingly tight and as a result, I had painful lessions on my wrists which became infected and in one place, the cuffs had eaten their way down to the bone. I was so thirsty and desperate that I finally decided to drink my urine. In some places, my flesh stuck to the handcuffs, making it excruciatingly painful to move my hands. I finally was able to cup my hands to catch the urine. As I urinated into the cupped hands, some of it splattered on the open sores. The intense burning was so excruciating that I screamed."

There are many stories like that of Menjivar, each describing its own horrendous form of violence. I have introduced such stories and discussed the "cult of death" to show the self-feeding nature of acts of violence in today's El Salvador. The ritualistic mutilations described are grisly ground for systematic inquiry. They suggest that the "political cult of death" could well be a theoretical framework in the study of modern political science.

11

Sacred and Deadly: The Church in El Salvador

On February 23, 1982, the Associated Press wire story, dateline Rome, Italy, was headlined "Pope Gathers Jesuits for 'Real Bawling Out'." It went on to explain that:

Pope John Paul II today was to launch a new purge of liberalism among the Jesuits at a closed-door conclave of the Roman Catholic order's officials from around the world.

The conservative pope is upset that many members of the Society of Jesus, the order's official name, have become political activists and support leftist movements in Latin America. . .

The sources said John Paul is also angry about many Jesuits' outspoken support for progressive causes within the church, including public opposition to the ban on artificial birth control and theological writings emphasizing the human rather than the divine nature of Jesus.

'We're going to get a real bawling out,' said a Rome-based Jesuit, who asked to remain anonymous.

The Jesuits, with 26,600 members, are the church's largest and most influential order. They run Vatican Radio, spread the gospel from New Zealand to Alaska, and have provided many of the church's most prominent liberal thinkers and militants including Rev. Robert F. Drinan and the Rev. Daniel Berrigan in the United States.''

As early as October 1981, the Pope had begun to tighten the reins by appointing his personal representative, Rev. Paolo Dezza, as head of the Jesuits — a move unprecedented in the 447-year history of the order's self-rule.

In July 1977, a Salvadoran group called the White Warrior Union, *Union Guerrera Blanca*, issued an ultimatum which was delivered by phone and in the mail to the country's newspapers and radio stations. All forty-seven Jesuit priests in El Salvador were ordered to leave the country by July 21st. Those failing to do so would be considered "military targets" by the underground organization, subject to systematic elimination. This was the opening round in an all-out war between anti-communists and liberal clergy in El Salvador. Even before this, in 1970, some right-wing groups identified the liberal clergy as dangerous and subversive. The clergy's influence was especially great in the university and among the poor whose political, social and economic causes they espoused. These progressive priests and nuns, many of whom were foreigners belonging to the Maryknoll or Jesuit orders, were considered "subversive conduits for dangerous notions from abroad."

In 1967, Ivan Vallier, professor of Sociology at Columbia University, wrote that "Religious elites and professional holy men hold a more distinctive place in history than warriors or kings." He adds that as guardians and interpreters of spiritual values and moral authority, they often emerged as ideological figures in times of crisis.

The Latin American Roman Catholic Church has always played a significant role in the government. From the very arrival of the Spanish conquistadores, the church and clergy were an integral part of the governmental system. Indians were baptized by the thousands (14,000 baptisms in one day in June 1529). The Indians did not understand the nature of their new commitment, thus ". . . severe physical punishment was often resorted to by the clergy in an endeavor to eliminate 'heathen' practices among these baptized, but scarcely converted natives. . . " The history of the church in Mexico is particularly interesting since that institution, by the end of the 19th century, had accumulated close to half of all the arable land in the country. Gifts by Indians to clergymen at confession led Thomas Gage, an Englishman who spent twelve years as a Catholic ecclesiastic in Latin America, to describe the Guatemalan clergy in a very negative light. Many, especially poor Indians, went weeks without confession as they saved up their donations. Property, such as coins or jewelry, found in public places was turned in to the clergy who kept it as church property. The priests claimed it belonged to the souls of the departed.

As with any institution, the church was always complex and fragmented; composed of progressive and reactionary, generous and miserly, cruel and kind individuals — all coexisting within the same structure. Churchmen both cooperated and vigorously fought against dictatorship. Opposed to birth control and other social measures, the church for centuries interjected itself in temporal matters. When clergymen became disillusioned with the machinations and heartlessness of the upper classes, they sometimes turned toward the mass of people and endowed the poor or the Indians with special and higher virtues. This happened especially in 16th century New Spain. In the post World War II decades, this "looking downward" at the lower classes, and attributing to them special virtues born out of suffering and poverty, was analyzed. Fredrick Pike's conservative conclusions are instructive in understanding this perspective. He suggests that "if churchmen concentrate exclusively on bringing about reform from below, by appealing to the lower mass for direct action, and ignoring the possibility of renewed cooperation with upper and social sectors, then along with Communists and other extremists, they seem destined to be a divisive force in society and can impede or disrupt the constructive endeavors of the state."

Others, however, have pleaded and exhorted for "progressive" behavior by Catholics. Pike quotes the prize-winning 1963 essay by Ricardo Talavera Campos, who in Lima, Peru, strongly condemned capitalism. Talvera called it a system of human selfishness and lust for profit, a system which cannot survive because it has no soul and is devoid of ideas and ideals. "Catholics," he said, "must jump from the sinking ships of capitalist society." Moreover, quoting Jesuit priest Angel Arin Ormazabel, Talavera exhorted the rich to give all their wealth to the poor. If they do not do so, he threatened, the poor would take control of the government and force the rich to give it up.

In Colombia radical priest Camilo Torres Restrepo left the church, joined a guerrilla group, and was killed by the Colombian army in an attack early in 1966. The "Rebel Priest" has since become a legend and a symbol of radical, Marxist clerical involvement in social movements. His photograph, the clerical equivalent of Che Guevara, hangs in many offices, classrooms, residences, and Parish houses.

Torres, son of a well-known aristocratic family, entered the priesthood, studied sociology at the University of Louvain in Belgium, then returned to Colombia fully committed to radical change. While Torres did not consider himself a communist, he firmly believed that an alliance between "progressives," such as himself, and communists or other Marxists was necessary. It was imperative, he felt, because in order for a just and pluralistic society to grow, power had to be wrested, usually by force and violence, from the privileged classes. His pursuit of "authentic humanism" rejected the possibility of a mass-based political party achieving victory at the polls. Another radical Catholic, Dom Helder Camara, Archbishop of Recife, Brazil, wrote in 1968:

> I respect those who, in conscience, feel themselves obliged to opt for violence, not the too easy violence of the drawing-room guerrilla fighters, but of those who have proved their sincerity by the sacrifice of their lives. It seems to me that the memory of Camilo Torres and of the Che-Guevara merits as much respect as that of the Pastor Martin Luther King.

Three years after Camilo Torres died, rifle in hand, fighting with guerrillas of the Army of National Liberation, a group of young Colombian priests called for ". . . an opening toward Marxism."

Throughout much of Latin America, the church has become divided between radical, conservative, and other clergy. Already in 1963, an article by M. Richard Shaull in the October *Theology Today* spelled out the complicated juxtaposition of Christians and communists. Speaking of the change which must come to 400-year-old anachronistic structures, the Princeton University theologian wrote that ". . . when Christians

become involved in movements which are working for such
change, they immediately discover that the Marxists were there
before them and are more prepared than anyone else for this
work." He argues against conflict between Catholics and Marxists, noting that social change in some areas "will have to come
as the result of joint effort of Catholics and Marxists."

In Central America, as elsewhere in this hemisphere,
this Christian-Marxist alliance often materialized. The revolutionary forces fighting against the Somoza dictatorship in
Nicaragua were particularly blessed with the cooperation of
radical clergy, including a number of American Maryknoll missionaries. In fact, there was one celebrated case of a Maryknoll
priest and nun who left the church, married, and joined the
guerrilla movement. In the post-Somoza, revolutionary Sandinista government, several high posts are held by clergymen. Three
ministers of state are Catholic priests — Ernesto Cardenal
Martinez, Minister of Culture; Miguel D'Escoto Brockman,
Minister of Foreign Affairs, and Edgar Parrales, Minister of
Social Welfare. Parrales told the Mexican magazine *Proceso*
that 85 percent of the Nicaraguan clergy side with the revolution.

A substantial part of Central America's clergy, as is true
in the rest of Latin America, have taken to heart parts of the
historical mandate issued by the 1968 Latin American Bishop's
Conference (CELAM) at their meeting in Medellin, Colombia.
Here the church stated that it must identify with the poor.
To this was added the influence of German theologian Karl
Rahner, the father of modern-day "theology of liberation,"
and the so-called "Pueblo Doctrine," which also reinforced the
progressive church.

In El Salvador, as in the rest of the region, the church was
divided and confused. Village priests, in the isolation of small
towns and farmsteads, lived with the daily suffering, disease,
and hunger of the peasants. Working class neighborhoods and
filthy, overcrowded slums were the domain of other clergymen.

The university represented yet another setting where the political and social problems of the country could be explored by radical priests.

Some of what the radical clergy is saying in Central America, Camilo Torres had already written in the mid-1960s in Colombia. In fact, I picked up a small flier at a meeting of the Central American clergy a few years ago, which reproduced a lengthy exhortation from Torres' book, *Revolutionary Writings*. It says more than any other analysis could of the role of radical clergy in El Salvador and Guatemala. Camilo (as he is familiarly called, even posthumously) wrote:

> All patriotic Colombians ought to place themselves on a war footing. Little by little, experienced guerrillas will appear all over the country. Meanwhile, we must be alert. We must gather arms and ammunition, seek guerrilla training, confer with one another, gather clothing, drugs, and provisions, and prepare ourselves for a prolonged struggle.

He urged a strategy of many small strikes against the "enemy." He advised weeding out the traitors of the movement. He predicted a long war and preached patience until the final victory. Then he exclaimed:

> Militants of the United Front: Let us make our assignments realized.
> For the organization of the popular class, until death!   For the unity of the popular class until death!   For the seizure of power for the popular class, until death!
> Unto death because we have decided to continue to the end.   Until victory because a people that is devoted unto death always obtains its victory.   Unto

final victory with the assignments of the Army
of National Liberation.
Not one step in retreat!   Liberation or Death!

This is quite a powerful and radical position for a clergy-
man. Most Catholic clergy have not come out explicitly for
such a radical course. Others have rejected entirely the revolutionary road to Christian justice. But death and violence are
very much a part of the church in all of Central America.
Father Jon Sobrino, a Jesuit priest affiliated with the Jesuit
University in El Salvador, wrote a fascinating piece in September 1980, entitled "Death and the Hope for Life." He stressed
that all of life in El Salvador is characterized by either death
or the hope for life. He states that the church has now "incarnated herself in this world of death." He quotes Archbishop
Romero who, two months before his murder, stated "I am
proud that Christians have mixed their blood with the blood
of the people." Father Sobrino then elaborates on the ways
in which the church has incarnated itself with the realities of
El Salvador — by being Indian, by being black, by being a woman. But he concludes that ". . . the depth of the incarnation does not come to light until one considers this further
type of incarnation: Sharing with the people of El Salvador
what is most profound and most basic — death."
      This revealing passage is significant because it overlaps
a series of realities and characteristics of the radical church in
today's Latin America. There is present in Camil Torres, in
Archbishop Romero, and in Father Sobrino, a legitimization of
death. It is seen as a positive virtue. We do not find avoidance
of death or its minimization, but rather the acceptance and
welcoming of death as a cleansing and binding experience. Also,
they reflect upon and have spoken of the parallel between Jesus
Christ's martyrdom on the cross, and the murder (sometimes
even called the "crucifixion") of the masses in Latin America.
Death in this analogy is not only spiritual, but has theological

and doctrinare legitimacy.

The reason that death is consistent with Christian values (the persecution and murder by the Romans and others is such an integral part of the Christian experience) is that the poor and the oppressed in Latin America are already the victims of death. Thus, death (or violence) to avert and dislodge "unjust death," represents a complex and rich logic. Sobrino, in fact, defines sin as "that which brings about death." Obviously, since Camilo Torres counselled people to arm and fight, "Counter-death" (such as justified acts of terrorism or self-defense) is really not death or sin to him.

I will not pursue here the philosophical, logical, or theological implications of this subject. However, the reader must be crystal clear on the position of an important segment of the progressive clergy. Death and violence are a vital part of "witnessing" — either by joining the masses in the suffering and subsequently becoming oneself the target and victim of death and physical suffering, or by inflicting violence on those commiting sins. Unless this is understood, much of the terribly confusing and apparently senseless violence involving the church or religious persons in Central America will not be understood. One must be careful here in not attributing the brutalization of clergy to "their own fault." That is absurd. However, within the various religious orders, and in the consciences of individual clergy, martyrdom is probably a significant factor. We know that becoming a martyr, dying, or suffering terribly is a great privilege among many fundamentalist Islamic seers. It is more difficult for Christians in the 1980s to understand that this phenomenon also has a place within their own faith.

Jesus said in the Sermon on the Mount, "Blessed are those who are persecuted for righteousness sake, for theirs is the kingdom of Heaven. Blessed are you when men revile you and persecute you and utter all kinds of evil against you falsely. . . Rejoice and be glad, for your reward is great in Heaven,

for so men persecuted the prophets who were before you."
Indeed, *Matthew* is one of the most pertinent books of the
New Testament. The worn pages of many Central American
missionaries' Bibles are at the beginning of the Holy Scriptures.
However, I saw the saying, "An eye for an eye and a tooth for
a tooth," scribbled on a calendar in a parish priest's office,
without the admonition of Jesus, "But I say to you, do not
resist injuries. . ."

Not enough systematic research has been done, nor even
good data gathered, on the church in El Salvador. How many
priests, nuns and lay persons are radicals? How many are
conservatives? Have any joined the guerrillas in the manner
of Camilo Torres? What is the role of the foreign clergy? How
many church people have been killed, tortured, or have disappeared? Even these elementary facts are not known, However, if the church and clergy of El Salvador in any way parallels
that of the rest of Latin America, it is a highly politicized and
fragmented institution. Most Americans, however, paid little
attention to the Central American clergy until two momentous
events occurred — the killing of San Salvador's Archbishop
Oscar A. Romero on March 24, 1980, and the murder of four
American church women on December 3, 1980. Both are tragic
reminders of the politicization of the Central American clergy.

Christopher Dickey's chilling description of the evening
of March 24, 1980, in San Salvador is in perfect character with
the tragedy of the Salvadoran Catholic Church.

> There is a hospital for the incurable in San Salva-
> dor. The archbishop lived there and often said even-
> ing Mass in the adjoining chapel.
>
> This night there was a special service, a memorial
> Mass for the mother of one of the few leftist pub-
> lishers still in the country. It was a pleasant evening,
> with the doors of the chapel open, as always, to let
> the cool night breeze circulate.

In his Sunday homily the day before, the archbishop had denounced the violence of both the left
and the government, but, as so often happened —
because there were so many more examples of
government violence to cite — he had seemed to be
attacking only the regime. More boldly than ever
before, he had made an appeal — a demand — for the
violence to end. He had directed his words to the
troops: 'I ask you, I pray you, in the name of God,
I order you to stop the repression! '

But this evening his words were quieter. He talked
of the need for any Christian to involve himself
in the world, despite the risks. 'He who wants to
withdraw from danger will lose his life,' said the
archbishop. 'But the person who gives himself to the
service of others will be like a grain of wheat that
falls to the ground and dies — but only apparently
dies, for by its death, its wasting away in the ground,
a new harvest is made.'

The archbishop prepared the Eucharist and raised
the chalice to God.

He never saw the gunman just inside the chapel
doors.

The gunman put a single bullet into Archbishop Romero,
instantly snuffing out his life. The political right is conclusively
blamed for the assassination.

Romero had been an increasingly outspoken critic of the
terror and government complicity in El Salvador's violence.
Moving from conservative to liberal, he enjoyed great support
and sympathy abroad. Human rights' groups in Europe and the
United States viewed him as the "apostle" of moderation and
justice. On February 17, 1980, one year before he died, the
archbishop had written a letter to President Jimmy Carter.
After urging Carter not to give military assistance to the

Salvadoran government and asking him to ". . . . guarantee
that your government will not intervene directly or indirectly
with military, economic, diplomatic, or other pressure to determine the destiny of the Salvadoran people," Romero outlined
the very essence of progressive Latin American Roman Catholicism. He said:

> In these moments we are living through a grave
> economic and political crisis in our country, but it
> is certain that it is increasingly the people who are
> awakening and organizing and have begun to pre-
> pare themselves to manage and be responsible for the
> future of El Salvador; only they are capable of
> overcoming the crisis.
> It would be unjust and deplorable if the intrusion
> of foreign powers were to frustrate the Salvadoran
> people, were to repress it and block its autonomous
> decisions about the economic and political path
> that our country ought to follow.
> It would violate the right, publicly recognized
> by the Latin American bishops' meeting in Puebla:
> 'The legitimate self-determination of our people
> that permits them to organize according to their
> own genius and the march of their history and to
> cooperate in a new international order'.

A brief analysis will reveal the complexities, innuendoes,
and historical significance of this statement. In the first place,
the allusion to "the people" is a recurring theme in the literature. This presents great difficulties because it is rare, if not
unheard of, for "the people" to make judgements about the
political future and destiny of a nation. More often than not,
the people, acting as individuals or families, make short-term

judgements about their own condition. The people, as Mr. Romero used the concept here, clearly means the political opposition groups, acting on behalf of the polity. The statement is ambiguous enough so that we cannot tell if he supported the position and policy goals of leftist insurgent groups. However, judging from his views on social policy and the future, it is safe to say that he privately welcomed a turn of events such as that which swept out the Somoza dictatorship in neighboring Nicaragua.

Second, the "intrusion of foreign powers" is explored. However, the archbishop was a fierce advocate of mobilizing the international human rights community and sympathetic governments on behalf of his suffering people. One colleague has noted that the "intrusion of foreign powers on behalf of the Salvadoran people" would, of course, be welcomed — indeed, it has been actively solicited by the *Frente Democratico* (especially in Europe, the United States, Mexico, and among Socialist nations since 1979). Finally, it is interesting to find a private citizen (although definitely a public figure) demanding guarantees of an intergovernmental nature from the American head of state. Presumably, under no circumstances, would or could President Carter guarantee that the U.S. government would not pursue its national interest in El Salvador through military, economic, diplomatic, or other means.

Nine months after the archbishop was buried in San Salvador, Americans woke up to another horror story involving the church. On December 4, over the first cup of coffee, millions watched the headline news story on the *Today* show — four pale, half-clad, dead females, lying in a lush, green grove of trees at the edge of a freshly-opened simple grave. U.S. Ambassador Robert White strode up and down the grave site, indignation radiating from his ruggedly handsome face, his greying hair disheveled. He repeatedly ran his fingers through his hair, trying to bring some neatness to it. There were three American nuns kneeling beside one body, their

hands folded in prayer, and much nausea at the site. There
were frightened, coy government officials, minor functionaries
(whose lives would depend on how they behaved at the scene
of this crime), talking with the U.S. ambassador. Present also
were peasant farmers, gingerly throwing sprigs of branches on
the half-naked cadavers, trying to preserve a touch of modesty
and decency in a situation of sheer debasement.

Ambassador White's cable to Washington on December 5
is a perfect summary of the events leading up to the discovery
of the murders. It is at once descriptive and revealing. Dealing
with a human tragedy in the time-worn bureaucratic tradition
of international diplomacy. Instead of using the full sixteen
letters and one space to spell out "American citizens," it
uses the ugly six-letter acronym "Amcits".

(Telegram unclassified, December 5, 1980)

DEPARTMENT OF STATE

Ref San Salvador 8480

E.O. 12065: NA
TAGS: CASC, PINS, PINT, SHUM, ES
Subj: More information on murder of four U.S. citizens

1.   Following is Embassy's reconstruction of the events
surrounding the deaths of four U.S. citizens — three nuns and
one lay missionary, two of whom were from the Maryknoll
Order.

2.   At approximately 1630 hours on Tuesday, December
2, two American citizens (Amcits) drove to the El Salvador
International Airport to pick up a party of four women returning from Managua. Only two of the women had been able
to obtain seats on the plane, and the other two had been

scheduled for a later flight. The first two travelers were driven by the Amcits to the City of La Libertad, located approximately 30 kilometers from the airport, where all intended to spend the night. After dropping off their passengers, the two Amcits returned to the airport to meet the two later arrivals. The second set of travelers arrived, and at approximately 1900 hours, all four talked with a group of Canadian missionaries at the airport.

3. The Canadian Missionaries left before the four Amcits. While driving from the airport to the main highway (the entrance road to the airport is approximately five kilometers long) the Canadians were stopped by uniformed individuals whom they identified as National Police. Their cars were searched and the Canadians were allowed to proceed. The Amcits had to travel the same route when leaving the BFD Airport.

4. To reach the San Francisco Hacienda from the airport entrance road one would travel twelve kilometers east on the main highway and then seven kilometers north on a secondary road. Between 2300 hours and 2400 hours on December 2, residents in that isolated area heard shots fired. Between 0700 and 0800 hours on Wednesday, December 3, the driver of a milk truck discovered the bodies of four women in a ditch beside a field close to the Hacienda. The nearest residence is located approx. 30 yards from the spot where the bodies were found. The local judge, whose job it is to identify bodies before they are buried, was notified at approx. 0830 hours and reached the site at approx. 0930 hours. He found several individuals already digging one common grave for the four bodies. Among the gravediggers were the village mayor (Joseph Olores Meledrez), two members of the National Guard (Sgt. Edgardo Rodrigeuz Correas and FNU Gaitan), three members of the "GMVIL Guard" (Arnoldo

Recind Aleman, and two others whose names are not recorded — all were described as Armed and uniformed and were probably members of the local commandante's unit), and four residents of the neighborhood (Alejandro Rivas, Joel Mesa, Mariano Rosales, and Pedro Realgeno). Since there were no documents on the bodies, the judge was unable to identify them, and the burial continued.

5.   Late Wednesday night or early Thursday morning an Amcit who had become worried about the four missing women discovered a smoldering car on the side of the highway approx. nine kilometers west of the airport entrance road. The car was totally burned and the license plates had been removed. Several hours later the Amcit identified the car as belonging to the mission women by the serial number of the motor. The car had not been sighted on that stretch of road earlier in the day. There are no houses near the spot where the car was found, but residents of the closest village reported seeing Hacienda police in the general area at about the time the car was set afire.

6.   On the morning of December 4 the Ambassador and Consul accompanied the Canadian Missionaries to the airport. While returning, they were notified by radio of the finding of four bodies near San Francisco Hacienda. After considerable searching, they reached the site at approx. 1330 hours. About an hour later the same judge who had seen the bodies on December 3 returned and gave permission to open the grave. The four bodies had been placed on top of each other under about six feet of earth. The face of the first body had been destroyed, perhaps by a high caliber bullet. The second was shot through the head, the third through the neck and breast and the fourth is believed to have been shot in the chest. According to the judge, one woman had been shot once, and all the others twice. The hands of the bodies were not tied, but one piece of cord was seen nearby.

Clothing of the victims was disarranged, and the underwear had been removed from two of the women.

7. A number of reporters witnessed the disinterment of the bodies.

/ Signed / White

The furor over the investigation into the murder of the Amcits is well known. The National Guardsmen arrested and charged with the murders were considered by some to be simply "stooges" — someone "up high" must have surely ordered this grisly crime. The Salvadoran government, reluctantly pushed into the arrests in the first place, steadfastly clung to the theory that they were "free-lancers" who had taken it upon themselves to kill the nuns. As with many Salvadoran crimes, the larger picture will probably never be known.

It is, however, intriguing to wonder why members of religious orders have become the targets of more and more violence. Bombings and shootings of Catholic clergy and lay persons have become more frequent in Guatemala as well — several Americans having lost their lives in recent years.

In El Salvador, one of the interesting speculations on the murder of the four religious women was that they were "not just nuns, but political activists." Conservative Senator Jesse Helms, for example, asked Sister Melinda Roper to provide a clarification on testimony at the hearings before the Foreign Relations Committee of the Senate on "The Situation in El Salvador." Sister Roper was asked about the statement by Maryknoll Sister Peggy Healy in a eulogy to the murdered women, that they supported the "Popular Project of the People of El Salvador." In a newsletter of the "Religious Task Force on El Salvador," where the article by Healy appeared, the "Popular Project" was defined as "The popular organizations of peasants, workers, slum-dwellers, students, and teachers who last April joined with the middle-class sectors to form the Democratic Revolutionary Front." In the same article, Sister Healy also identified the "Popular Project" as "the opposition to the present government." Helms clearly was implying that the nuns were identified by Salvadoran security people as supporters of the left, even of the guerrillas. While it was not implied that the killings were justified, Helms wanted to underscore the possible "political motivations" which could have led to the violence.

One does not have to agree or sympathize with Helms to point out that indeed Maryknolls and Jesuits, as well as other progressive orders in Latin America, have been suspect in the eyes of conservative political groups. The Senate hearings also alluded to the August 1980 issue of *Maryknoll* magazine which focuses on the Cuban Revolution. It shed an extremely favorable light on Castro's government and even quoted him as saying:

> We propose an alliance between Christianity and Marxism. The human objectives of Christ and Marx, each within his own philosophy, are the same. We cannot speak about the next world, but in this one we can have complete concurrence, with fraternity and solidarity.

Sister Roper concluded her testimony by answering a question about the use of violence to bring about justice, saying, "Many desire peace, but not at the price of justice for the poor — this is a false peace."

This theme is supported by Salvadoran Marxist guerrilla leaders, one of whom stated to Mexican reporter Mario Menendez, that the church has had "an extraordinary social sensibility and great political proximity with the democratic and revolutionary forces."

Rafael Minjivar, in his excellent analysis of Salvadoran politics, goes so far as to see the church as a tactical instrument in the Central American War. "The CIA," he observed, "counsels not to attack the church as an institution, but instead establish a division between progressives and those who are not. . . ." He continues that in his view, having identified God to communist priests who are betraying the evangelical message of Jesus Christ, it would then be acceptable to kill or persecute the progressive clergy.

In El Salvador, the church today is an organic, vital part of political battles.

I have tried to bring together in this chapter material which sheds light on the role of the contemporary Catholic church in Latin America's revolutionary climate. It appears that a major portion of the church has opted for revolution and even a tactical alliance with Marxists. Camilo Torres' teachings and writings are sometimes actively cited as the relevant reference point for action. At other times they serve as a subtle backdrop for ideological decisions on the correct line to follow vis-á-vis armed struggle.

What is terribly significant, and this point seems to have been missed by almost all recent analysts of the Salvadoran struggle, is that both progressive clergy and conservative (or at least anti-communist) political forces have, by and large, taken an absolutist position. Fidel Castro said some years ago, "Inside the revolution — everything; outside the revolution — nothing." The clergy in Latin America, it appears, have been placed on the sharp edge of the same dilemma. To support radical reform, the poor and the peasants in a country convulsed by civil war, (such as Nicaragua or El Salvador) must identify with the leftist opposition. Moreover, the historical record, radical church doctrine, and even the pronouncements of Fidel Castro himself, attest to the likely alliance between Marxist political groups and progressive clergy. The likelihood of being tagged as a "communist" is double in the case of

Jesuits and Maryknolls. It is an even more acute problem for clergy who have worked with the Sandinistas in Nicaragua; a closer investigation will show that there are numerous Nicaraguan ties between clergy killed in Guatemala and those killed in El Salvador. One can make sense (in the perverse logic which is currently gripping Central America) of the attack against clergy, without either justifying or condoning such actions. Both the right and the left are telling church people what radical anti-war groups and black militants told Americans in the 1960s: "If you're not part of the solution, you're part of the problem." The terrible agony of Catholic clergy in El Salvador today is that the left and the right have drastically different interpretations as to what "the problem" is and, thus, what "the solutions" are. Violence is both a symptom, and perhaps the very disease of Salvadoran politics.

12

The Disturbing
Election of 1982

"El Salvador resembles Vietnam, " the February 17, 1982 *The New Republic* states, "because at the rate things are going it will shortly become another Communist country allied with the Soviet Union." The Vietnam analogies thus continue. The confusion, disgust and exasperation of a seemingly hopeless puzzle of El Salvador's problems, have slowed America's intervention into Salvadoran affairs. In 1982 *The New Republic* argues that there were roughly four options available for solving this horrendous problem: The first was to simply concede the country to the guerrillas, end all U.S. support, and then contain the leftist regime, which had gained power. A second alternative was to push for negotiations and arrange a coalition between the revolutionaries and the government. The third option was to place top priority on winning the war militarily, even if it meant using U.S. forces in El Salvador. Finally, the United States could pressure the existing Salvadoran government to hold elections and expand land reform and human rights' programs.

On March 28, 1982, elections were held in El Salvador. The decision to hold an election was reached after months of consultation, both within El Salvador and with the United States. El Salvador's President Duarte, himself frequently a victim of past corrupt elections, said, "It would be the first free election in the history of this country." The United States hoped that Duarte and his Christian Democrats would win.

The Salvadoran guerrillas ridiculed the elections by labeling them, "By the right, for the right; by a minority, for a minority." The guerrillas promptly called for a boycott, threatening to cut off the fingers of, or kill those who voted.

U.S. Senator Edward Kennedy of Massachusetts objected to the plan, arguing that conditions in El Salvador were not conducive to free and open elections. The Senator's views reflected those of liberals in the United States, as well as officials of several Latin American and European governments.

The forthcoming election was not cast against a backdrop of security and stability. The hulls of burned-out buses accumulated along the dusty roads of northern Salvadoran provinces. Barefoot children in ragged clothes poked through the charred remains of the buses for salvageable items. The rhythmical to and fro batttle between government troops and guerrillas continued. Such were the scenes in El Salvador in that portentous March of 1982. Violence and intimidation were everyday facts of life.

I met and talked with a man in Costa Rica, who had lived near San Salvador and had then left with his family a few days before the elections. He was on his way to a permanent exile, his face reflecting confusion and despair.

"It became clearer that as each day passed," he said as he stared into the bottom of his coffee cup, "that our chances of being hurt or killed were about equal whether we voted or not."

The guerrillas roaming his region had left word that anyone voting in the election would be considered sympathetic to the "reactionary government in power."

"Attacks against buses and skirmishes became more frequent. We were frankly frightened," he continued. "A few political candidates passed through and they told us we should vote to save the country."

This refugee sensed that government agents were adamant in their demand that people turn out for the election. "No one ever told me I would be killed or beaten, " he said. "We talked about it with friends and concluded that it might be dangerous not to vote. We were really trapped in an impossible situation."

"But what did you want to do? " I asked. "What did you feel would help bring the country out of its crisis? "

"Nothing," he responded in a hopeless tone. There are no words to express the depths of his pessimism. "I'm not a political person, but I know enough to see that the guerrillas would never concede in an election what they've expected to win in battle. Why should they? "

The United States government was aware that the electorate was trapped between a rock and a hard place. Efforts were made to simplify the process and to avoid the usual Latin American technique of dipping voter's fingers into indelible ink at the time they cast their ballots. A team of international observers was assembled. They would soon roam the polling places and participate in the ballot count to insure a modicum of honesty in the process.

The scenario, which both Washington and the Duarte government hoped for, was risky. Salvadorans, it was said, were tired of violence and repression. The efforts by moderate and conservative Christian Democrats to implement reforms would be an incentive for voters to back the political middle. Since no leftist groups presented themselves as candidates, the choice would be between conservatives, rightist candidates, and the Christian Democrats. It seemed reasonable to expect that Duarte and his party's candidates would do well. Thus, the beginnings of a politically centrist government could be reasonably expected.

As the campaign began to unfold, the vigor and determination of conservative groups surprised many. Especially disturbing was the prominent role assumed by one candidate, retired Major Roberto ("Major Bob") d'Aubuisson.

Intensely youthful and surrounded by a mystique of violence, d'Aubuisson was precisely the wrong person to win the contest. Washington began to worry, and Duarte himself became extremely concerned.

D'Aubuisson, "an attractive campaigner with a winning smile and a promise to step up the war against the guerrillas," was gaining momentum. "The guerrillas are destroying us with their guns," he said, "and the Christian Democrats with their laws." He drew record crowds at festive rallies, with his boyish smile and his easy style, while being guarded by an uncompromising contingent of heavily armed body guards.

Jim Goodsell of the *Christian Science Monitor* called d'Aubuisson's newly created political party, Alianza Republicana Nacionalista (ARENA), "the hottest political force in the campaign." The thundering oratory of ARENA militants seemed always to be taking place in an atmosphere festooned in blue, white and red banners, mariachi bands playing animated "rancheras," and street vendors hawking their ices, flowers, sweets, and multi-colored drinks.

A rally at the National Gymnasium in San Salvador featured all the makings of the campaign. D'Aubuisson's eyes darted defiantly, but nervously, around the gym, ever aware that he was the clearest symbol of the hard line; a worrisome problem for Washington.

The strains of his campaign song, "Tremble, tremble, communists" reverberated through the hollow building. On the podium in front of him lay a large watermelon, d'Aubuisson's visual aid, to remind voters that he viewed Duarte as green (the color of the Christian Democrats) on the outside, red (communist) on the inside. "Christian Democracy and communism," he thundered, "are one and the same thing." Adding, "Our struggle may cost lives. It won't be easy, but it is the only way to do away with our enemies. They must go or we will go."

D'Aubuisson's emergence as a key figure on the political scene was, to say the least, disturbing. A former Army major, he was linked to the death squads— *escuadrón de la muerte.* The 38-year-old d'Aubuisson had been drummed out of the army after he plotted a coup against the government in 1978. The U.S. and Salvadorans also accused him of excessive brutality in pursuing the war against leftist groups. Always a controversial figure, he was called "pathological" by former U.S. Ambassador Robert White. White also accused him of engineering the assassination of the Roman Catholic primate of San Salvador, Archbishop Oscar Romero in 1980. D'Aubuisson was reputed to have threatened the use of napalm against the guerrillas. He said on several occasions that if elected, he would "exterminate" the guerrillas within three months. The ARENA marching song says "El Salvador will be the tomb where we bury the reds." No one doubts that ARENA's solution is based on violence.

Senator Edward Kennedy, in a senate speech on March 25, 1982, also alluded to d'Aubuisson's public threats against the U.S. charge d'affairs in San Salvador. D'Aubuisson claimed himself to be responsible for a shooting attack on the U.S. Embassy in March 1981.

A business associate of d'Aubuisson, Ricardo Sol Meza, was detained (with Hans Christ) and questioned about the January 1981 murder of American labor advisors Mark Pearlman and Michael Hammer. Most of this evidence comes from papers seized in El Salvador in May of 1980. One of the documents is a detailed account of arms purchases and expenses (including haircuts, girls, meals and payments to contracted men). The diary belonged to Captain Alvaro Rafael Savaria, considered to be d'Aubuisson's right-hand man.

In the days before the March 28 election, a concerted effort was made by those opposed to the election to accomplish one of several objectives. First, it was hoped that second thoughts would force a postponement of the voting. If that were not possible, and indeed it was extremely unlikely at the eleventh hour, then perhaps adverse publicity might convince Salvadorans to cast their ballots for more moderate candidates, probably Duarte's Christian Democrats. Barring that, it was considered important to signal to Salvadorans that d'Aubuisson must not be elected president. Finally, a vigorous public debate might induce Salvadoran politicians to quickly move toward negotiations with opposition forces, after the election.

A political solution through negotiation has been a possibility for a long time. France and Mexico moved to recognize the guerrillas as a "legitimate political force" several years ago. Then on February 21, 1982, in a speech delivered in Managua, Nicaragua, Mexican President Jose López Portillo politically outlined a detailed proposal for negotiated settlement in El Salvador's conflict. President López also suggested a means of alleviating tensions between the United States and Cuba and Nicaragua. Pointing to the difficulty of elections without negotiation or negotiation without elections, López Portillo offered Mexico as a good faith arbitrator for a political solution.

On March 15, 1982, former moderate junta member Colonel Adolfo Majano, now exiled in Mexico, endorsed the negotiation process. Without guerrilla participation, he noted, the upcoming elections would be "meaningless." The bespectacled, scholarly-looking young officer indicated that despite a strong Marxist component in the guerrillas, in his estimation, they would not want to become part of the Soviet bloc. The guerrillas' offer of unconditional negotiations was an opportunity to test their goodwill. Others, including Robert S. Leiken of Georgetown University and French President Francois Mitterand, also urged some form of negotiation.

The mystique surrounding negotiations in El Salvador is similar to the Israeli's trying to negotiate with the Palestine Liberation Organization, (the PLO). Two days before the election, former President Duarte said that he rejected the idea of talking "with those who carry arms," because they want a place in the government which they have not been able to win on the battlefield or, for that matter, at the ballot box.

More conservative groups in El Salvador and in the U.S. claimed that negotiations were simply a tool used by the left to drive itself into the government. Once entrenched, they would seize power and establish a Marxist regime. The guerrillas themselves never spelled out their reason for a sudden willingness to talk, when they had so staunchly refused to do so in earlier years.

The complexity and controversy of the negotiations was underscored by the scheduled meeting of the Socialist International in Caracas, Venezuela, on February 24, 1982. This is an association of democratic socialist political parties. When Nicaragua's Sandinistas asked to attend the meeting with observer status, socialist leaders from Costa Rica, Venezuela and the Dominican Republic protested, arguing that the Marxist-Leninist position of the Nicaraguans was not compatible with democratic socialism. The meeting was abruptly cancelled. Many wondered how Marxist revolutionaries and conservatives in El Salvador could possibly sit down and talk, if even socialists were worried about subversive radicalism and revolutionary guerrillas.

The U.S. pre-condition for talks with the guerrillas was an unconditional end to the violence. U.S. Secretary of State Alexander Haig told the U.S. House Foreign Affairs Committee that "the parties who wish to responsibly negotiate a solution to the tensions must commit themselves to a termination of the activities which are the cause of the tension." Unimpressed, the House voted 393 to 3 in favor of a non-binding resolution calling on the Reagan administration to negotiate with all parties without preconditions. In early March, the U.S. House resolution signalled that if negotiations preceded and accompanied the elections, the voting would have a better chance of being one of several positive steps toward peace.

As Congress pressed for negotiation and the White House proceeded with plans for an election, violence errupted again in El Salvador and an election day blood bath loomed ahead. Everyone was aware that an overwhelming rightist victory in the elections would make the job of extracting cooperation from Congress more difficult.

President Reagan warned that such a victory would be extremely displeasing to Washington. At the same time, the State Department's Dean Fisher said the United States hoped for post-election talks which would bring some leftists back into the mainstream.

Pre-election violence continued unabated. D'Aubuisson himself became the target of attacks. Two days before the election, ARENA headquarters in San Salvador was machine-gunned and bombed. While the perpetrators were probably a leftist group, d'Aubuisson hinted it might have been the Christian Democrats. The next day, March 27, d'Aubuisson had to abort a helicopter trip, making an emergency stop when guerrillas attacked the town of San Sebastian. His helicopter came under fire and, later that same day, his convoy was attacked by terrorists with hand grenades. D'Aubuisson was slightly injured by bomb fragments.

Christian Science Monitor editor, Jim Goodsell, reported an intense campaign to disrupt the elections with guerrillas concentrating their fire, especially on transportation. In three days, over forty buses were burned and more than fifty people were killed. Then suddenly, all became quiet.

On Sunday, March 28, dawn broke with the sweet song of birds. A damp, gentle breeze blew and the anticipation of the impending election day was in the air. The stench of burning tires, crackling gunfire, and helicopter gunships were in evidence once again.

In some places, notably the city of Usulutan, (the country's fourth largest) the gunfire was part of a major battle which raged over several days. Elections in a few places had to be cancelled because there was no way to keep polling places open. Several hundred peasants who had trekked for hours into Usulutan, their dusty faces streaked with sweat, were turned away and several were seriously injured as guerrillas sought to end the balloting.

In the country as a whole, however, the turnout at the polls was large. After the count, 1,185,185 ballots of an eligible electorate of roughly 2 million had been cast. These figures were remarkable. However, the distribution of the votes was far from promising. The election had pitted six political groups against one another. The Christian Democrats received roughly 41 percent of the vote, giving them 24 seats in the 60-member constituent assembly (seven short of a majority.) D'Aubuisson's ARENA with 29 percent got 19 seats, the Popular Salvadoran Party, 3 percent with one seat; the National Conciliation Party received 17 percent of the vote and 14 seats; Democratic Action, 9 percent and two seats; and the Popular Orientation Party, one percent with no seats.

The results of the elction were distressing to Washington. ARENA and d'Aubuisson had formed a coalition which would, in effect, give them the power to influence, or even dictate post-election policies. However, the Reagan administration was euphoric over the huge voter turn-out. This seemed to confirm their claim that Salvadorans wanted ballots, not bullets.

An exhausted President Duarte couldn't believe the outcome.

He was out-voted by the very groups against which he had been pressing reforms. In the days after the election, he defiantly stated, "I think that the people believe that I should stay in the government." Meanwhile, U.S. Ambassador Dean Hinton buttonholed Salvadoran politicians, urging them to moderate, to be inclusive and to heal wounds.

First, Ambassador Hinton urged that d'Aubuisson not be named interim president of El Salvador. Second, he counseled rhetorical restraint, particularly dangerous in the U.S. view, was the intention by the right to try Duarte and other Christian Democrats for "treason." He urged that the winners not practice confrontational politics and thus divide the non-Marxist, non-revolutionary forces. He also warned that the loser should not talk about fraud as is common after every Latin American election. It would undermine the entire purpose of having an election in the first place.

One point of leverage for moderates was that the rightist coalition lacked the two-thirds majority to effectively govern. While earnest, sober politicians agonized over how to structure El Salvador's new government, Salvadorans left in droves for their Easter week holidays. José Duarte flew to Costa Rica. "Everyone's gone to the beach," one diplomat observed.

On April 29, the final profiles of a new government finally took shape. Alvaro Magaña, a 56-year-old lawyer and economist, considered a political independent, was elected provisional president. A Friedman economist who had received his Master's degree in 1955 from the University of Chicago, Magaña seemed to be a reluctant candidate for president. In a *New York Times* interview he said, "I don't think of myself as a balancing power. I prefer to believe that the political leaders and the people consider me somebody that is going to try to make things work." He saw himself more as an administrator, a chairman of the board, than as a political leader.

A survivor of the 1956 Andrea Dorea ship disaster, Magaña has been a political pragmatist. His supporters call him a liberal, but the right wing has grumbled that he is a leftist and the revolutionary left dismisses him as another U.S. puppet, and an instrument of Salvadoran Oligarchs. A small bust of President John Kennedy adorns his bank office. Horn-rimmed glasses and a receding hairline give him a harried look. "I'll be worn out by the end of the year, for sure," he lamented in May of 1982.

Magana's administration was handed the challenge of presiding over a government of "National Unity". Most observers agreed that this was surely an euphemism. Only a week earlier, one defiant ARENA leader explained the sweep of all assembly posts, which the coalition of rightists gave itself, in this way: "We did this today to show the United States Embassy that they are not going to tell us what to do."

On May 3, 1982, Costa Rica's *La Nación* published an extensive analysis of the new Salvadoran government. The full-page picture of ex-president Napoleon Duarte on the front page quoted him as saying, "We left El Salvador on the road to stability." Duarte's quiet insights include his assertion that his government did a marvelous job of maintaining a viable subsistence economy in a country at war. When *La Nación* reporter Victor Hugo Murillo asked if negotiations with the left should now begin, he stated conclusively: "Now less than ever there is nothing to negotiate because now there is a president."

Duarte argued that the elections have produced a government which is legitimate and anchored on a popular mandate. "No one can negotiate this away," he asserted.

The new and tenuous Salvadoran government's cabinet included ARENA on the far right, the "Centrist", National Conciliation Party (PCN), and the Christian Democrats. The first two parties obtained four cabinet posts each and the Christian Democrats got three. This hybrid government seemed peculiar in at least one regard; under great pressure from the military, the PCN had divorced itself from ARENA and joined the Christian Democrats in electing Magaña president. ARENA's d'Aubuisson had wanted the job at one time.

As a concessionary and bargaining gesture, d'Aubuisson was given the presidency of the constituent assembly. D'Aubuisson, no novice to hardball politics, has a powerful tool with which to rule: "Decree No. 3".

Decree No. 3, put in the hands of the assembly, had extremely broad governing powers. It gave the assembly the authority of naming top officials in the provisional government; the right to ratify all cabinet appointments; all legislative authority; the power to write a new constitution; and, the initiative in organizing new national elections.

By the end of May, these powers were wielded scythlike to mow down the reform program.

The worst fears had come true when a Salvadoran deputy acknowledged that the next step might be a break-up of the farm cooperatives which had been formed during phase one of the agrarian reform. It seems as if the clock was turning backward. A dismayed U.S. Congressman, Michael Barnes, Chairman of the House Inter-American Affairs Sub-Committee said, "These actions seem to confirm that the wrong guys won."

A report on Salvadoran elections prepared by the Jesuit Central American University in San Salvador in June of 1982 seemed to indicate that the total ballots cast in El Salvador had been greatly inflated. To be precise, it suggested that only half as·many people had actually voted. It seemed that the ratio of votes given to each political party was preserved, but the numbed doubled in order to show a massive rejection of the left. In a secret pact, it was agreed by the parties that a large voter turnout would impress the world, and give temporary breathing space to the new government. Already, the presidium of the Socialist International meeting in Bonn, West Germany on April 2 had ridiculed the elections by saying, "The so-called elections provided no solution to the terrible ravages of the civil war." After the elections of March 28th, the killings again increased. The government had changed, El Salvador had not.

At the time of this writing, the solution to El Salvador's political crisis is still elusive. We saw earlier that four choices seemed possible — a leftist victory, a military solution, elections, or a negotiated settlement. These are by no means distinct and clear options. Each is kaleidoscopic, containing infinite angles, colors, nuances and shapes.

For example, it is clear that even those who most vigorously oppose the Salvadoran right-wing are fragmented into more narrow groups. Some favor a leftist revolutionary victory, others a centrist solution, still others a truly progressive military strong-man. Supporters of the right are also in disarray; some want to crush and eliminate the left, others preferring to wean away the moderates from the guerrillas; some are against any socially progressive reforms, others favor them. The left itself is more divided than it currently appears. Moderate backers of the guerrillas, such as Social Democrat Ungo, now exiled in Mexico, believe they could be given a fair role in a revolutionary government. Hard liners such as FPL leader Salvador Cayetano Carpio or the ERP's Joaquin Villalobos surely will not compromise their goal of a Revolutionary Marxist government.

This pluralism in organization, thought and action was precisely what led to elections as the mechanism for rebuilding or, perhaps, building up El Salvador's new government. By denying the extreme left access to power because they would not participate in the elections, it was felt they could be embarrassed and neutralized. The discredited and violent right would also suffer humiliation. The logical result would be an invigorated center which could then form a position of power and negotiate with the moderate left and right. But as I've described it, the scenario went sour. One of the remarkable things about recent Salvadoran politics is the assumption by many parties of the middle and by U.S. conservatives that the U.S. must be firm, uncompromising and violent in crushing the guerrillas. Progressive revolutionaries want the U.S. not only out of El Salvador, but out of all Central America. When these views of the American role are scrutinized, it is crystal clear that American foreign policy for all intents and purposes has no supporters in El Salvador!

Clearly for U.S. liberals and Salvadoran moderates, the American role since the 1979 coup has been too soft on human rights' violations. It has "winked at repression in the name of reform." None of the governments since the fall of the Romero dictatorships have satisfied the standards of human rights, reform and democracy. Congressional doubts, the mobilization of El Salvador support groups, marchers and demonstrations against U.S. policy on campuses and in Washington have increased steadily over the past three years.

Conservative Salvadorans and many Americans have felt that U.S. policy was playing into the communists' hands. Conservative groups in El Salvador are deeply irritated by AID development experts, hostile press and demanding Congressmen trying to "straighten out" their country's problems. America's policy has been a hindrance in solving El Salvador's violence because it has given Marxist guerrillas the impression that American public opinion would rather have another Nicaragua than a right-wing regime.

The left loathes the United States for providing just enough aid to the government to prevent the revolutionaries from winning a decisive victory and thus delaying the day when the guerrillas march into San Salvador.

The election itself was a U.S. aid package, delivered at a crucial time when the junta was faltering. It injected new life into the Salvadoran government and forced the guerrillas to temporarily re-think their tactics. But late in the summer of 1982, nothing fundamental had really changed in San Salvador, in the villages of the provinces nor in the lush, green coastal plantations. It seemed more like an expedient excuse to delay a real solution.

13

New Directions and Old Problems

The young banker poked his fork at the food on his plate. He carefully maneuvered the peas around the rice, as he pondered aloud the situation in El Salvador. "Can a government with over one hundred years of roots buried in its soil be reformed by U.S. pressure?"

"I've read the Marxist analysis," he said, not waiting for my answer, "and it's the only coherent explanation of why we've ended up in this hell. No one else seems to have an explanation of the past or a plan for the future." Bewildered, he took a bite of dried cake and washed it down with a gulp of soda water. His appetite for food, and for discussing

179

politics, was gone. But like the banker's need for food, the need for change in El Salvador and the compulsion to talk about that need had been only temporarily satiated.

As this man pointed out, El Salvador's main problem is that it clings to its past. The social-political structures of a hundred or more years ago no longer work. These structures were acceptable when human rights and participatory government were nothing more than far-off European and American notions, but now the eyes of the world are focused on El Salvador's erratic social and political situation. El Salvador appears to have one foot in the past, and the other uncertain where to set down. Though the traditional way of governing is outmoded, the new is still not within grasp. El Salvador's tumultuous transitional period invites a host of antagonists who promise cure-all governments. Groups from both the left and the right promise, and sometimes deliver, rural and urban development, and social programs. These improvements camouflage the groups' quest for power and the violent means they use toward that end.

Violence has already hardened the alternatives of the Salvadorans and created irreconcilable social and political conflict. The tens of thousands who have been killed or tortured prove how tenaciously El Salvador clings to its faded past. Merely changing governments cannot dislodge attitudes held for hundreds of years. The problem is much more serious because very powerful, conservative Salvadorans still believe in traditional means of governing. Conversely, the revolutionary socialists believe that nothing from the past worked well. Such divergent beliefs leave no common ground for compromise and for change.

Yet, we should not make conclusions about El Salvador based on U.S. social-political structure. The situation in El Salvador is not much worse than it is in many Latin American countries. The chaotic, violent situations in these countries are not as widely known, because the United States has not participated so publicly in them. But the violence in Argentina, Chile, Cuba and Uruguay is as rampant as it is in El Salvador.

Countries such as Haiti and Honduras are actually worse off economically and socially than El Salvador. The Guatemalan guerrillas are far more ferocious than the Salvadoran guerrillas. As well, the international repercussions of the Salvador situation seem minuscule compared to those of the Nicaraguan revolution, which is potentially more dangerous because it may drag Cuba, the United States and Russia into the conflict. Mexico is yet another country that has such grave socio-economic problems, resulting from its size, its limited oil resources and its common border with the United States, that it could become an El Salvador magnified a hundred times.

As in other Latin American countries, the entrenched attitudes of generations of Salvadorans precipitate violence and inhibit change. However, an observer of the situation should not allow the violence to overshadow the fact that attempts are made by various groups to form a quasi-capitalist, or non-Marxist, politically responsible government.

"No amount of deceptive reformism will distract us from what must be done," one pamphlet reads. The pamphlet could have been printed by either the left or the right since both groups oppose true reform.

Despite the unwillingness of both groups to yield to each other and to change, the United States tried and failed to manipulate the outcome of events in Central America. The U.S. failed because there were few opportunities to implement change and also because U.S. officials were just as divided and uncertain on what to do as the Salvadorans were.

Since 1979, the United States mainly has supported the El Salvador government with military and economic assistance. Former President Carter and President Reagan both certified that conditions in El Salvador were "improving."

However, Carter pressured for greater human rights by withholding aid to El Salvador. Reagan said in 1982 and again in 1983 that conditions were improving, especially in agriculture, despite continued reports of torture, heavy fighting and suspension of reform measures. Both administrations were criticized by the left and the right. But the left seems to prefer the Reagan administration and the ultra-conservative Salvadoran government because they support the left's contention that "Nothing has changed."

In addition to presidential certification or censure, the U.S. Congress mandates twice yearly documentation that human rights and social conditions improve. After all, can torture, murder and the effects of reactionary policy be indexed to determine if conditions are improving? If this were possible, who would be entrusted to tally the casualties?

If the United States was seriously attempting to remedy the problem in El Salvador, they might fully support the Frente Democractico. This party offers an alternative to the bloodshed, yet such outspoken critics of El Salvador as Senators Edward Kennedy and Christopher Dodd, and Congressmen Tom Harkin, Gerry Studds and Clarence Long balk at giving their full support, probably because their constituents would oppose it. Conservative critics have even suggested that these Congressional foes of U.S. policy, particularly its military assistance to El Salvador, are indirectly aiding the guerrillas and hoping that the left will gain control.

United States' groups who are sympathetic with the Salvadoran left openly try to sway the Congress and American public opinion to the side of revolution. "The most important variable in terms of influencing the outcome of the struggle in El Salvador is the U.S. mass popular response to U.S. policy," writes Rick Kunnes in his introduction to *El Salvador: No Middle Ground.*

"A very broadly-based, U.S. anti-war movement is literally essential for the Democratic Front to win," Kunnes states.

Where would U.S. action be directed? Would it cut off aid to the present junta, now the Magaña government, which Kunnes says would help the Revolutionary Front win?

The author advocates that no stone be left unturned in the support of the liberation of El Salvador. "There is no alternative to unqualified support for liberation and no middle ground in El Salvador."

Because there is no middle ground, many Americans are uncertain about what action to take, and ambivalent about getting involved. The United States clearly fears that international Marxist revolutionary movements will eventually threaten the United States. If El Salvador fell to extreme leftists, it might become a heavily militarized link in the chain, beginning with Cuba and continuing through Nicaragua. A Marxist El Salvador might cause revolutionary action in neighboring Honduras, Guatemala, and even Costa Rica and Panama. If such a chain reaction occurred, the Panama Canal and Mexico's oil fields would be extremely vulnerable. From there, one might wildly imagine an effort to subvert the large Hispanic community in America, and to appeal to radical black groups, as Fidel Castro did in the 1960s and the 1970s. Radical student groups would also be used to undermine American stability.

As farfetched as this scenario may seem, many Latin Americans believe it is inevitable. "Venezuela has always been the ultimate objective of Cuba," according to a high-ranking Venezuelan air force officer. "Cuba has no oil and we are the largest producer. El Salvador is one of the roads leading to the Gulf of Maracaibo, Venezuela's oil producing zone."

The officer's tight fitting shirt bulged as he shifted in the uncomfortable cafeteria chair. He said that he had seen communism's effects when he flew to Cuba as part of an airlift to bring people off the island. "When we landed there was an interminable silence, an almost drugged crowd lining the runway," he said. "The Cuban militia marched the passengers into our transport. The passengers sat stone silent, not moving, staring straight ahead."

"After the plane took off, sandwiches and pop were offered, but no one accepted them. Then we made an announcement: 'We have just left Cuban airspace'."

"Pandemonium broke out. People screamed, several of them had involuntary bowel movements, others urinated in their clothes." The officer's eyes were moist and his nostrils flared as he recalled the intense experience. He was visibly shaken as he cupped his hands around a mug of black coffee, nervously slopping it on his stiff, starched shirt.

Many Salvadorans believe, as this air force officer does, that communism and socialism are evil. Thus the war in El Salvador is closely watched by all Latin American leaders. These leaders silently endorse American policy supporting a rightist victory. Progressive Latin Americans, of course, see the U.S. as the major obstacle to social change and development.

But what about the plight of the peasants, the workers, the unemployed? Can the United States assure a better way of life for these people? Should they try?

Conventional U.S. policies such as development loans and technical assistance have not helped correct problems in El Salvador. During the 1970s, millions of dollars were spent on schools, health centers, purification of water, electrification, road improvement and nutrition programs. These efforts have not substantially improved the quality of life in El Salvador because technical aid does not change political and civil rights. Technical aid, no matter how well funded or spent, will not provide freedom of speech, freedom of press or freedom to organize.

The fact that U.S. aid has changed almost nothing makes many Americans cynical. "We don't know how to build new societies," a development specialist said, "and that's the bottom line of what El Salvador needs." A bureaucrat likened the situation in El Salvador to a drowning man treading water in the middle of the ocean. Sitting behind piles of technical reports, the bureaucrat explained that American policy was a "confused patchwork of socialism and capitalism, an eclectic mix that people have a hard time understanding."

Another bureaucrat said that government plans called for a three percent increase in the per capita income of peasants, or for one additional year of school for the urban poor. "Who the hell is going to get very excited over that? " he exclaimed in frustration. "We can't promise a chicken in every pot and we certainly don't promise a car in every garage. We don't even promise a garage! " He said that the socialists promise a new society and a new man. "Now that's something to sink your teeth into," he mused, stopping for a fresh piece of pineapple and a shoe shine.

Neither American nor Salvadoran policies noticeably improve the average Salvadoran's life, and these programs do not yield support for the government either. A feeling of suspicion, secrecy and coercion caused by various militant regimes hangs in the air. Because of this ill-feeling and due to the opposition to reform, by both the extreme right and extreme left, officials are almost apologetic in implementing reform programs.

People working with these projects are asked to take great risks, to expose themselves to untold dangers, with no offer of protection from the government. Military governments are tremendously disadvantaged in being secretive, suspicious, and internally divided between reactionaries and reformers, so support for reforms and optimism for their workability are not part of Salvador's political base. In such an atmosphere even technically sound programs such as the United States' flounder.

The greatest difference between the Salvadoran government and the revolutionary guerrillas is symbolic. Both groups use force to gain, or to maintain their power. Government officials are characterized as being overweight officers, wearing dark sunglasses and a humorless expression. They are seen driving heavily-reinforced armoured vehicles around the dirt and rubble of the cities and villages. Television and newspapers pick up on these frequently-seen characteristics, juxtaposing them with the struggle in Central America.

The left, by contrast, is depicted as a group of bright, young, energetic do-gooders. They tuck their longish hair under colorful caps, wear tennis shoes and beads, have personalized arm patches and carry bright banners. The left is characterized as a mixture of Robin Hood and the boy scouts. They are adventurous, live a simple life and work in great camaraderie with the peasants.

The characterizations of the left and right are not as silly as they appear. Many Salvadorans accept such depictions. In Nicaragua, after the fall of Somoza, public mobilization spawned revolutionary art, especially large murals and inspirational sloganeering. Nicaragua blossomed with a revolutionary spirit that had millions participating in accomplishing national goals, unlike the "carnival atmosphere" of the solidarity movement in the Polish military government. Different techniques and symbols are used and, of course, there are different government objectives. Most importantly, though, Nicaragua gradually moves masses of people toward societal and political ends, instead of forcing immediate change.

It is debatable whether the so-called reform juntas or current Salvadoran government could use this centrally-based style of leadership. However, the mood preceding the El Salvador election of March 1982 seems to suggest that mobilization could yield improved social and political conditions. This assumes that the regime would pursue genuine reform.

If the Salvadoran government were to instill a sense of pride and belonging to those participating in government programs, the problems in El Salvador might be resolved. The government might provide a "people's uniform," caps, patches, slogans and songs. It might also encourage celebrations, parades and demonstrations in support of social reform programs. And instead of shrinking the size of the international advisors who run the programs, the government could greatly expand its size.

What impact would three thousand U.S., European and Latin American volunteers working to improve education, public health, recreation and agriculture have? "Just think what would happen if people from Los Angeles and Houston, from Caracas and Berlin were killed or tortured by government troops? Imagine the dilemma of the guerrillas in attacking villages or carrying its violent action into the cities? " a bureaucrat asked.

The failure of U.S. policy is that it is carried out so quietly and bureaucratically. For the past three decades, the United States has simply pumped more money and more military aid into El Salvador when the situation got more violent. As one economist said, "We shrink back into secluded offices and we pray a lot."

We are so ambivalent about our approach that we cannot possibly make visible, energetic commitments. For example, we don't directly involve civilian, volunteer and government personnel in monitoring human rights. Perhaps, we could pair a foreign volunteer with a Salvadoran from a humanitarian agency such as the Green Cross, which distributes medicine and conducts medical care. In July of 1982, a Salvadoran Green Cross volunteer was placed on an old fashioned wheel rack and stretched. He was strung up and his testicles were squashed in a vise, a technique referred to as the "Carter." The man was severely beaten and forced to inhale lime. Would this man have been treated as brutally had he been paired with a Swiss or American partner? If the foreigners were tortured, the Salvadoran government would have to deal with the wrath of foreign governments. Perhaps, that would be enough to eliminate a great deal of the violence.

It is clear that our silent economic, social and military technique has not worked in El Salvador. The American government has not even been able to protect its own citizens. U.S. Consular officials lackadaisically investigated the murder of four assassinated church women and two development experts murdered in El Salvador. It is futile for the U.S. to stubbornly pursue marginal reforms and to try to forge more participatory politics using economic and military aid alone.

An acquaintance of mine complained, "The U.S. is a terrible ally— it's a real liability. Your technical and social reform programs don't work. You ask governments to cut themselves loose from the old anchors, to take life and death risks, then when things get sour, you don't know how to see us through the mess. All you can think of is more military aid, but of course not risking American soldiers. Washington doesn't have the support at home to take creative risks."

A former development advisor said that U.S. efforts were technically sound, but politically naive. "Our government just doesn't have a complete picture," he said, sipping a Harvey Wallbanger and wiping the sweat from his face. He said that some of the U.S. reforms worked on nutrition, others on improving cattle or grain, another on sewage and water treatment, and yet another concentrated on public health. "Hell, all those things don't amount to a hill of beans if the government we're dealing with is run by a corrupt bunch of incompetents." The beads of sweat rolled down his face as he motioned to the waitress for a refill. "We claim that it's not within the Congressional mandate to 'interfere politically', yet that's precisely what needs to be done. We've got to step on a lot of toes, our staff people must be freed to talk to the media. We've got to cultivate a mystique, a passion for development." And, he added feeling the cool tonic of his drink on an unbearable Washington summer day, "We've got to greatly increase our level of committment."

I think the former development advisor's observations about Central America are right. And I think that unless the U.S. can reach a consensus on how to improve the situation in El Salvador we should consider pulling out. It is unlikely that the conservative establishment, the Congress and the Reagan administration will radically alter American policies. What is more unlikely is that thousands of U.S. volunteers will risk death or torture in an ever-expanding U.S. involvement there. But the largest drawback is that we have no plans or mechanisms for effectively reversing the custom of violence as a means to power in El Salvador.

One military expert suggested that state department or special observers be stationed at every security facility to monitor government atrocities. He said that he'd give the observers a two-way radio to the embassy on which they would report any misconduct. "If the Congressional critics really mean what they say they should each send down a couple of their staff people as part of the monitoring service. Imagine a thousand or so staffers with walkie-talkies and standard human rights' monitor sheets! "

All this seems inconceivable, if not incredibly farfetched. Barring more conventional changes, what constructive role can the United States play? If we pulled out of El Salvador, several things could happen. The left could take power. We could probably tolerate this government. After all, we maintain diplomatic relations with Hungary, Zambia, Angola, China and even Pol Pot in Cambodia. We also tolerate extreme right governments, such as those in Uruguay, Uganda, Pakistan, South Africa and Bolivia. The Salvadoran extreme right might bring off a successful revolution if it were unfettered by the press, the Congress, and the Reagan administration and the families of U.S. citizens killed there.

A third alternative would be to continue to muddle through, suffering international scorn and criticism. If this is our solution, our troubles have just begun. As many as two hundred people die each week in the guerrilla war in neighboring Guatemala. In Honduras, guerrillas blow up plants and attack police. And the terrible economic-social conditions in Costa Rica threaten to bring violence to that tranquil country as well.

The situation in El Salvador is only the beginning of our problems in Central America. The outcome could end with Salvador Cayetano Carpio, the hardened, committed Marxist, as president or dictator. Can our economic policies eliminate the stagnation, unemployment and budget deficits in Central America? During this period of great impatience and desperate need for change, can moderate military regimes or middle-of-the-road reforms be realistically suggested as alternatives to the traditional way of governing? Or will the old method of giving assistance and demanding change from the top down, rather than participatory assistance and governance, continue to be used? Is it as Professor Juan de Mairena notes, "The common tendency of man is to accept the expedient as truth."

As of this writing, in late July, 1983, the Reagan program for El Salvador and Central America seems to be solidifying in a "hard line" approach. The United States appears to be embarking upon a course all too reminiscent of American policies followed in the early Vietnam years. The recent dispatch of warships to both coasts of Nicaragua, U.S. Army and Special Forces war games in Honduras, and increased emphasis on military aide to El Salvador, Guatemala and Honduras all seem to refute Ronald Reagan's words, given in his July 26th press conference, that his policies were not a step toward a Vietnam-like war. In that same news conference Reagan argued that Americans who "understand the situation" agreed with his policies. The President claimed that economic and humanitarian aid to Central America outweighed military aid by a ratio of three to one. In that argument, Reagan did not point out that military aid was increasing at a much greater pace than economic and humanitarian aid. Nor did the President indicate that he supported the Defense Department's call for more U.S. military advisors in Central America. One thinks back to 1963. At that time the United States had 70 military advisors in Vietnam. Within a matter of months that figure jumped to several thousand. When those advisors came under Viet Cong attack, the U.S. Marines were landed to protect the advisors. Marine combat units fanned out, taking up "defensive" positions. America's war in Vietnam had begun.

American policies during the Vietnam years and Reagan policies in present-day Central America are frighteningly parallel. In this writer's opinion, the current American administration is casting a political and military scenario for Central America which must lead but to two alternatives: the United States will gradually involve iteself in a Vietnam-type war or, failing to gain popular American support for such a war, the United States will pull out, abandoning that sad land to a long and bloody conflict between the extreme left and right.

Within recent weeks President Reagan established a 12-member bipartisan commission to study and recommend long-range policies toward Central America. The commission has been hailed by some as a positive effort. The appointment of Henry Kissinger to head the commission undoubtedly is designed to give that body the prestige and influence lacking in present policy-makers of the Reagan administration.

One should not hold out too much hope for the Kissinger commission. It begins its efforts with severe limitations. And its true purpose is suspect. There is strong reason to believe that the Kissinger commission was established by the Reagan administration as a psychological gambit to ease its problems with Congress over increased military aid to Central America. It can be argued, as well, that the commission is not really bipartisan, but weighted heavily on the side of the hard-liners. Certainly Henry Kissinger's own record in Vietnam and as U.S. Secretary of State shows a consistent hard line unmarked by a change in direction. Whether that direction has been

right or wrong is not the question. The question is whether former Secretary Kissinger is prepared to modify that position.
And such a modification seems remote.

The Kissinger commission begins with two additional re-
strictions which in themselves seem fatal. First, the commission
will not actually formulate U.S. policy. It only can make recom-
mendations. This writer doubts that the Reagan administration
will alter its course substantially no matter what the findings of
the commission. Secondly, the Kissinger commission will not
present its findings until sometime in mid-1984. By that time
the Reagan policies towards Central America and El Salvador
will have been so firmly established that one doubts if any sug-
gestions at that late date will have any impact whatsoever on
the course of events.

No doubt the remainder of this decade will answer most of
the questions raised in this book. No matter what the answers,
it appears that much money, effort, heartache and bloodshed
will be spent before there is a final solution to the problems in
El Salvador and Central America. What America's role will be
in this transformation depends upon U.S. policy today. That
policy is cause for deep concern. Only the U.S. Congress and
American public opinion are able to exert sufficient pressure
on the present administration to alter its hard line posture.
Failing this, the future for El Salvador and Central America
darkens. For as of this moment, the United States seems driven
upon an unalterable course toward its second Vietnam.

— end —

BIBLIOGRAPHY AND NOTES

Chapter I

IN THE GRIP OF VIOLENCE

No one can understand the horrors of Latin American political torture and human rights' abuse without reading Jacobo Timerman's *Prisoner Without a Name, Cell Without a Number,* (New York: Knopf, 1981). While Timerman narrates his Argentine ordeal, it conveys so vividly the atmosphere in other Latin American countries. For an excellent overview on El Salvador, one should read *Revolution in El Salvador: Origins and Evolution* by Tommie Sue Montgomery (Boulder: Westview Press, 1982). The book deals sympathetically with the plight of El Salvador's people and is especially strong in analyzing the ins and outs of the revolutionary forces. A thumbnail background with a strong section on the Salvadoran Armed Forces can be found in Howard I. Blutstein et. al. *Area Handbook for El Salvador* (Washington: U.S. Government Printing Office, 1971).

Chapter Notes

p. 1, paragraph 1: Quotations by Salvadorans other than from printed sources will be anonymous or under fictional names to protect the sources. This was an ironclad understanding under which I had to operate.

p. 3, paragraph 1: *Diario Latino,* November 28, 1980.

p. 4, middle page: The Colonel Choto incident was related by an American who lived close by.

p. 5, paragraph 1: T.D. Allman, "Rising to Rebellion," *Harper's,* 3-81, pp. 31-50.

p. 5-7, The accounts of the abduction have been reconstructed from newspaper accounts and interviews.

p. 7, 4th line: *Diario Latino,* November 28, 1980.

p. 10, paragraph 4: The secretary's callous remark reveals a great deal about the use and acceptance of violence in El Salvador.

p. 12, paragraph 1: Defending your own property is not uncommon in Latin America where the police are, at best, unreliable. When my grandmother's house was broken into in Colombia, it took two days to just get the police out to look.

p. 13, paragraph 2: The notion that strong and stable government is all that wonderful is denied by the hundreds of thousands who have fled such diverse countries as Cuba, Uruguay, and post-Allende Chile.

p. 13, paragraph 3:   Sandy Pollack, "Quagmire in Central America," *Political Affairs*, May 1982, pp. 35-40.

Chapter II

DOMESTIC, REGIONAL OR GLOBAL CRISIS?

For those who have never read a congressional hearing I highly recommend the one entitled *U.S. Policy Toward El Salvador*, a compilation of the March 5 and 11, 1981 hearings before the House Subcommittee on Inter-American Affairs. The testimony for and against the Salvadoran government and the almost surrealistic confusion and conflict in testimony is quite instructive. A small book, *El Salvador: Una Autentica Guerra Civil* by Mario Menendez Rodriguez, is a must for those who read Spanish. It was published in 1981 by the University of Costa Rica. This book gives interesting details about the diverse and sophisticated level of organization of the opposition forces and makes for somber reading. For those needing an "overview" of the regional crisis in Central America, I recommend Richard E. Feinberg's article, "Central America: No Easy Answers" in *Foreign Affairs*, Summer 1981. Feinberg concludes that the U.S. should not react in panic to revolution in Central America, but rather should attempt to settle its differences with Nicaragua as a means to solving the crisis in El Salvador, while at the same time seeking a negotiated solution in El Salvador as an aid in normalizing relations with Nicaragua's Sandinistas. Finally, two articles from the magazine *The New Leader* are very helpful. Paul E. Sigmund's piece, "Pressing for Peace: The Next Step in El Salvador," (April 5, 1982) concludes that the U.S. should recruit other Latin American countries into a leadership role to promote the negotiation process between rebels and the Salvadoran government. Irving Louis Horowitz's article "Thinking Aloud: Neoliberalism: Poland, Si, El Salvador, No," (May 3, 1982) is fascinating. Pointing out that U.S. liberals have lost their nerve, Horowitz castigates liberals for their timid demand for human rights in Poland while berating American policy in Central America, in particular El Salvador.

Chapter Notes

p. 15, paragraph 1: *Newsweek*, May 21, 1979.
p. 16, bold type: The headlines are from *Newsweek, The Christian Science Monitor, U.S. News and World Report, The Des Moines Register, The Omaha World Herald*, and *The Economist*.
p. 21, paragraph 1: Mario Menendez Rodriguez, *El Salvador: Una Autentica Guerra Civil*, (San José: Editorial Universitaria Centroamericana, 1981), p. 18.
p. 21, paragraph 2: Menendez, p. 69.
p. 22, paragraph 1: Menendez, p. 72.
p. 22-23, last paragraph: Menendez, p. 127.

p. 23, various quotes: Menendez, p. 131, 173-74, 185, 187.
p. 24, paragraph 2: Gene Hogberg, "Turmoil in Central America - Here's Why," *The Plain Truth,* May, 1981.
p. 24, paragraph 4: *Diario Latino.*
p. 24, paragraph 5: *Diario de Hoy.*
p. 25, paragraph 1: *U.S. Policy Toward El Salvador,* Hearings before the Subcommittee on Inter-American Affairs of the Committee on Foreign Affairs, House of Representatives, Ninety-Seventh Congress, March 5 and 11, 1981. The editor of *Diario de Hoy* was Mr. Enrique Altamirano (p. 163), General Knight's statement is on pp. 312-313. Col. Dicken's statement is on pp. 209-210.
p. 25, paragraph 2: Menendez, p. 188.
p. 26, top of page: A very powerful critique of liberalism and El Salvador can be found in Irving Louis Horowitz, "Neoliberalism: Poland, Si, El Salvador, No," *The New Leader,* May 3, 1982, p. 10-13.
p. 27, top of page: Robert Leiken is cited in "Central America: Soviet Hit List . . . or Wish List," by Daniel Sutherland, *The Christian Science Monitor,* May 7, 1981, p. B2.
p. 27-28: W. Scott Thompson, "Choosing to Win," *Foreign Policy,* No. 43, Summer 1981, pp. 78-83.
p. 28, paragraph 1: *The Christian Science Monitor,* July 18, 1980.
p. 29, paragraph 1 and 2: Leonel Gomez and Bruce Cameron, "El Salvador: The Current Danger," *Foreign Policy,* No. 43, Summer 1981, pp. 71-78. This article contains the best discussion on the role of corruption in motivating the Salvadoran officer corps.

Chapter III

SPANIARDS, DICTATORS AND WIZARDS

If I had one book to read about this period in El Salvador's history, it would be Thomas P. Anderson's excellent *Matanza: El Salvador's Communist Revolt of 1932,* (Lincoln: University of Nebraska Press, 1971). Not only is this a well-researched piece, eminently readable, but it also describes the most significant event in the country's recent political life. For those who read Spanish, John Baily, et. al. *El Salvador de 1840 a 1935* (San Salvador UCA Editores, 1978) is good. For a fascinating view of El Salvador and Central America through the lens of the year 1918, one can read Dana G. Munro, *The Five Republics of Central America* (New York: Oxford University Press, 1918). This book was sponsored by the Carnegie Endowment for International Peace. Chapter IV (Nicaragua) and V (El Salvador) are very instructive. Germán Arciniegas wrote a book published in 1952 called *The State of Latin America* (New York: Alfred A. Knopf, 1952). It is a witty, anecdotal essay which gives an excellent "feel" of the mood in Central America. Arciniegas is a great storyteller and therefore from Chapters XIV and XV which deal with Central America and the Caribbean, one learns a great deal about the idiosyncratic nature of Latin America (and Salvadoran) politics. Since politics and economics are so closely intertwined, those who read Spanish and want greater depth of understanding for the importance of coffee in the life of El Salvador's development, I recommend Abel Cuenca's valuable *El Salvador: Una Democracia Cafetalera.* (Mexico: Costa-AMIC, 1962).

Chapter Notes

p. 32-34: The description of old El Salvador is adapted from Julio C. Estampas del Viejo San Salvador, (El Salvador: Imprenta Cuscatlan, 1978).
p. 34, paragraph 3: Hubert Herring, *A History of Latin America,* (New York: Alfred A. Knopf, 1968, pp. 47-48.
p. 34, paragraph 4: Helen Miller Bailey and Abraham P. Nasatir, *Latin America: The Development of Its Civilization,* (Englewood Cliffs, New Jersey: Prentice-Hall, 1968), p. 99.
p. 35, paragraph 2: Charles Gibson (ed.), *The Spanish Tradition in America,* (New York: Harper Torchbooks, 1968), p. 108.
p. 36, paragraph 2: Miller & Nasatir, p. 448.
p. 37, paragraph 2: Herring, p. 437.
p. 39, paragraph 1: Victor Alba, *The Latin Americans,* (New York: Praeger, 1969), p. 138.
p. 39, paragraph 2: Abel Cuenca, *El Salvador: Una Democracia Cafetalera,* (Mexico: Costa-AMIC, 1962) and Luis de Sebastián, "Las Raices de La Revolucion," paper presented at the 1982 meeting of the Latin American Studies Association, Washington, D.C.
p. 41-42: Germán Arciniegas, *The State of Latin America,* (New York: A. Knopf, 1952), p. 291.
p. 42, paragraph 1-3: Thomas P. Anderson, *Matanza: El Salvador's Communist Revolt of 1932,* (Lincoln: University of Nebraska Press, 1971), pp. 98-138.

Chapter IV

THE ARMED FORCES BECOME POLITICAL: 1948-1960

A good journalistic perspective on El Salvador can be obtained from Paul P. Kennedy, *The Middle Beat: A Correspondent's View of Mexico, Guatemala, and El Salvador* (New York: Teacher's College Press, 1971). Kennedy was a New York Times correspondent in Central America. It covers the late 1950s and early 1960s. Interviews and descriptions convey useful glimpses of the mood in El Salvador during this period. Hector Dada Hierzis, *Le Economia Salvadoreña y la Integración Centro-Americana: 1945-1960,* (San Salvador: UCA-Editores, 1978) is the best analysis of economic forces at work in the postwar period. Dada was until recently a key civilian political figure and member of the early reform junta. Two excellent studies of the critical "soccer war" are William H. Durham, *Scarcity and Survival in Central America: Ecological Origins of the Soccer War* (Stanford: Stanford University Press, 1979) and Thomas P. Anderson, *The War of the Dispossessed: Honduras and El Salvador, 1969* Lincoln: University of Nebraska Press, 1981). In both of these books one gains tremendous insights not only into the "soccer" war, but one also comes to understand the relationship between overpopulation, land shortage and underdevelopment, the three main root causes of El Salvador's current violence. For Spanish readers the best analysis of how the military became political is Rafael Guidos Vejar, *El Ascenso del Militarismo en El Salvador* (San Salvador: UCA-Editores, 1980).

Chapter Notes

p. 45, paragraph 1: Edwin Liewen, *Arms and Politics in Latin America* (New York: Praeger, 1967), p. 92.

p. 46, paragraph 2: Hubert Herring, *A History of Latin America*, pp. 484-485.

p. 46, paragraph 3: See Jorge Arias Gomez, *Farabundo Marti, Esbozo Biografico* (San José: EDUCA, 1972) for a good analysis of the 1930s.

p. 47, quotation: Cited in Harry Kantor, *Patterns of Politics and Political Systems in Latin America* (Chicago: Rand McNally, 1969), p. 113.

p. 48-49: Kantor, p. 115.

p. 51-52: Howard I. Blutstein et al. *Area Handbook for El Salvador,* (Washington: U.S. Government Printing Office, 1971), pp. 20-21. See also Roque Dalton, *El Salvador* (Havana: Cuba, 1965) for a radically different interpretation.

p. 52, paragraph 1-2: G. Pope Atkins, *Latin America and the International Political System,* (New York: The Free Press, 1977), p. 207.

p. 53, paragraph 1: Cited in Rogelio Sanchez, "La Guerra Desplazada," *Avance*, May-Aug. 1970, p. 12. It appears to be a paraphrase of Blutstein, p. 22.

p. 53-54: Pope Atkins, p. 289.

p. 54, last paragraph: Herring, p. 485. See also Eduardo Colindares, *Fundamentos Economicos de La Burguesia Salvadoreña,* (San Salvador: UCA-Editores, 1977).

p. 55, paragraph 1: Kantor, p. 117.

p. 55, paragraph 1: Peter Calvert, *Latin America: Internal Conflict and International Peace,* (New York: St. Martin's Press, 1969), p. 168.

p. 56, paragraph 1: Kantor, p. 117.

p. 56, paragraph 2: Kantor, p. 129.

Chapter V

THE RULES OF THE POLITICAL GAME

Latin America's "rules of the game" in politics are at best perplexing. A very useful perspective is given by Douglas A. Chalmers in "Parties and Society in Latin America" *Studies in Comparative International Development,* VII, No. 2, Summer 1972, pp. 102-128, because he sorts out the societal dynamics as they affect politics. Charles W. Anderson in his book *Politics and Economic Change in Latin America* (Princeton: Van Nostrand, 1967) offers an intriguing formula by which "power contenders" demonstrate their diverse "power capabilities" to obtain a share of the political action. The "capabilities" can be violence, votes, and other politically relevant assets. Marxist interpretations of the situation differ quite radically, stressing "dependency" and U.S. intervention as well as class struggle and capitalism. See for example Gustavo Lagos and Horacio H. Godoy, *Revolution of Being: A Latin American View of the Future*, (New York: Free Press 1977); an intriguing book which focuses on "development" and "deterioration" as key conceptual reference points. The only generalization one can make is that a consistent thread of military preponderance in politics has worked against the structually weaker and disunited civilian actors. Brian Loveman and Thomas M. Davies, Jr. *The Politics of Antipolitics: The Military in Latin America* (Lincoln: University of Nebraska Press, 1978) is a very instructive resource book. It includes extensive excerpts from Latin American military pronouncements which give a direct "feel" for how the military views politics.

Chapter Notes

p. 61-62, paragraph 2-4:   Douglas A. Chalmers, "Parties and Society in Latin America" in *Studies in Comparative International Development*, VII, No. 2, Summer 1972. pp. 102-128.
p. 63, paragraph 1:   See my paper "Politics, Violence and Reform in El Salvador," Occasional Paper, Dept. of Political Science, Iowa State University, 1981.
p. 64, last paragraph: "U.S. Policy Toward El Salvador," Hearings before the Subcommittee on Inter-American Affairs-Committee on Foreign Affairs, House of Representatives, March 5 and 11, 1981, p. 67.
p. 65, top of page: ibid., p. 200.
p. 65, paragraph 1:   Steve Frazier, "After the Revolt: Nicaragua is Plunged into Economic Crisis under Near Anarchy," *Wall Street Journal*, Sept. 15, 1981, p. 1.
p. 66, pp. 2:   Professor Machada uses a fictional character to concoct all manner of "Wisdoms." Antonio de Machado, *Juan de Mairena*, (Berkeley: University of California Press, 1963), p. 7.

Chapter VI

ON THE EVE OF THE 1972 ELECTION

There are two books which provide a comprehensive overview to this period. Stephen Webre, *José Napoleón Duarte and the Christian Democratic Party in Salvadoran Politics 1960-1972*, (Baton Rouge: Louisiana State University Press, 1979) is good because it's detailed. Webre does an excellent job of tracing the ever changing subtleties of Salvadoran political factionalism. Unfortunately, the study provides less insight into Duarte the man; his feelings, likes, dislikes, tastes, habits and flaws. Alastair White's *El Salvador* (New York: Praeger, 1973) is a solid piece of research — an amalgam of primary and historical sources and the author's personal interpretations and analysis. He spent time in El Salvador prior to writing the book in the mid 1960s and early 70s. Like so many books about the Third World written by First Worlders, it is dedicated "to the poor people of El Salvador." Coincidentally, a friend of mine who was working in a poor neighborhood of San Salvador some years ago found one poor family which got the book — it was nailed with a spike to their shack by the ravine which serves as the outhouse. ("The paper is too hard," one of the kids living in the house told my friend). David Browning's book *El Salvador: Landscape and Society* (Oxford: Clarendon Press, 1971) is a carefully done, historical geography of El Salvador.

Chapter Notes

p. 68, paragraph 1: Stephen Webre, *José Napoleon Duarte and the Christian Democratic Party in Salvadoran Politics, 1960-1972,* (Baton Rouge: Louisiana State University Press, 1979), p. 142.
p. 68, paragraph 2: ibid, p. 149.
p. 70, paragraph 2: Victor Alba, *The Latin Americans,* (New York: Frederick A. Praeger, 1969), pp. 357-358.
p. 70, last paragraph: Alastair White, *El Salvador,* (New York: Praeger, 1973), pp. 107-108.
p. 71, last paragraph: ibid, p. 213.
p. 72, quote: ibid., pp. 214-215.
p. 73, paragraph 2: ibid., p. 201.
p. 75, paragraph 2: This was the comment of a Salvadoran student living in Chile in 1971.
p. 76, paragraph 1: I am grateful to Prof. Richard Millett for his insights into the critical nature of the 1972 election. Millett is one of the most knowledgeable American scholars working on Central America.

Chapter VII

BREAKDOWN: THE END OF CIVIL POLITICS IN THE 1970s

Elections are often a boring and overly complicated aspect of political history. El Salvador's elections are no exception, but Ronald H. McDonald (no relation to the hamburger man) has a good chapter (Ch. 5) which covers El Salvador, in his book *Party Systems and Elections in Latin America,* (Chicago: Markham Publishing Co. 1971). For an interesting look at El Salvador on the eve of the March 5, 1967 election, one can read *El Salvador: Election Factbook,* Washington, D.C., Institute for the Comparative Study of Political Systems, 1967. The publication has lots of useful background information and concludes that "There is a trend toward more responsible democratic elections; votes are counted with less fraud," and "The military as a group seems to be less given to political activity . . ." How times change!   David R. Reynolds' book *Rapid Development in Small Economies: The Example of El Salvador* (New York: Praeger, 1967) is helpful but frustrating because it's over generalized and doesn't address the key issues of development in El Salvador: top down, dependent capitalism. An excellent thumbnail sketch — a libretto if you will — of El Salvador and U.S. policy there is "El Salvador, U. S. Interests and Policy Options," Issue Brief Number IB 80064, Congressional Research Service (CRS), updated 5/28/80.

Chapter Notes

p. 78, paragraph 1: interview, San Salvador.
p. 79, paragraph 1: Webre, op. cit., p. 141.
p. 80, paragraph 1: interview, San Salvador.
p. 80, paragraph 3: Ronald H. McDonald, *Party Systems and Elections in Latin America,* (Chicago: Markham, 1971), p. 262.
p. 81-82: This narrative is reconstructed from Webre, op. cit., Latin American newspaper accounts and interviews.
p. 88-89: The Rodriguez affair is reconstructed from *The New York Times,* 1976, May 17, 18, 28, and September 22, November 24, December 22.
p. 89, last paragraph: Ronald H. McDonald, "El Salvador: The High Cost of Growth", p. 397 in Howard J. Wiarda and Harvey F. Cline, (eds.) *Latin American Politics and Development,* (Boston: Houghton Mifflin, 1979).
p. 90, paragraph 2: "El Salvador, U.S. Interests and Policy Options," Issue Brief Number IB 80064, Congressional Research Service, (CRS), 5/28/80.
p. 91, paragraph 2: ibid.
p. 92, paragraph 1: I am grateful to Holly Burkhalter, formerly on Congressman Tom Harkin's staff, now on the House Select Committee on Human Rights, for her insights and assistance in obtaining documents on Human Rights in El Salvador.

Chapter VIII

OCTOBER 15, 1979: THE COUP D'ETAT AND THE ARRIVAL OF THE PROGRESSIVE JUNTAS

Sometimes a book comes along at just the right time. Former U.S. Ambassador to El Salvador Frank J. Devine's *El Salvador: Embassy Under Attack* (New York: Vantage Press, 1981) is just such a readable, modest, insightful book. Devine served in the U.S. Embassy in San Salvador from 1977-1980, that is to say the critical time when El Salvador entered the revolutionary phase. Another sensitive and useful book is Plácido Erdozain's, *Archbishop Romero: Martyr of Salvador,* (Maryknoll, N.Y.: Orbis

Books, 1981) which is translated from a 1980 Spanish version. The author is an Augustinian priest who worked with the Archbishop in San Salvador. I'm citing this book here rather than in the chapter on the church because it does so lucidly narrate the disintegrating situation in El Salvador during the late 1970s until October 7, 1980. "Death As a Way of Life" by Christopher Dickey, *Playboy*, Oct. 1981, pp. 109-186 is very readable. Finally I highly recommend T.D. Allman's article "Rising to Rebellion," *Harper's*, March 1981, pp. 31-50 because Allman has such a fresh and indignant approach to writing about this region.

Chapter Notes

p. 100, paragraph 1: Frank Devine, *El Salvador: Embassy Under Attack*, (New York: Vantage Press, 1981), p. 140.
p. 100, paragraph 2: ibid., p. 137.
p. 101, paragraph 1: ibid., p. 136.
p. 101, paragraph 4: ibid., p. 135-136.
p. 102, paragraph 2: ibid., p. 137.
p. 103-104: Plácido Erdozain, *Archbishop Romero: Martyr of Salvador*, (Maryknoll, N.Y.: Orbis Books, 1980), pp. 66-67.
p. 105, paragraph 1: Devine, op. cit., p. 146.
p. 108, paragraph 1: from interviews in El Salvador.
p. 108, bottom: Erdozain, op. cit., p. 55.
p. 112: Attacks against the U.S. Embassy and the Ambassador's residence have occurred repeatedly in El Salvador. This narration is from Devine. So as not to confuse the reader, let me stress that attacks have taken place from the leftists as well as from the rightists.
p. 113, paragraph 2: Devine, p. 150.

Chapter IX

THE CARTER/REAGAN POLICIES:
REFORM, REPRESSION OR REVOLUTION?

This is a vast subject. Surprisingly, there aren't many good books to recommend. *Symposium on El Salvador and U.S. Policy in the Region*, FACHRES, University of California, Berkeley, 1981, is a helpful collection of comments and discussions among experts. *Revolt in El Salvador*, Pathfinder Press, 1980, is a little pamphlet of interesting Socialist observations of El Salvador of which Nancy Cole's "Carter's Secret War Against El Salvador" is sort of classic because it's in the anti-Vietnam war genre. Another classic example, this one illustrating why U.S. policy is erratic, is a little Senate Executive Report No. 96-31 titled "Nomination of Robert E. White," a transcript of the Senate Foreign Relations Hearing on February 27, 1980 to confirm White as the new U.S. Ambassador to El Salvador. The clash of ideas and ideologies in the process of these hearings is very, very instructive. Central America at the Crossroads, Hearings before the

Subcommittee on Inter-American Affairs of the House Committee on Foreign Affairs, Sept. 11 and 12, 1979 is also interesting. Assistant Secretary of State for Inter-American Affairs, Viron P. Vaky's testimony is a great review of the official U.S. policy in Central America. A six-page "special section," "Showdown in El Salvador" in the April 1981 issue of *World Press Review* is a varied menu of short pieces from British, German, Brazilian and Spanish newspaper sources. Finally for the person wanting great detail (but some bias) – *El Salvador Land Reform, 1980-81,* OXFAM/ America, March 1981, is quite detailed.

Chapter Notes

p. 114, "El Salvador: Agrarian Reform Sector Strategy Paper." US-AID, 7-31-81, (Draft).
p. 115, paragraph 1: "Nomination of Robert E. White," U.S. Senate Committee on Foreign Relations, Feb. 27, 1980.
p. 115, paragraph 2-4: Mario Menendez, *El Salvador: Una Autentica Guerra Civil,* (San José-EDUCA, 1981), p. 16 and p. 45.
p. 116, top: ibid., p. 45.
p. 117, top: One said, "That's why the constitution guarantees the right to bear arms." See Mr. David Garst's testimony to the Committee on Foreign Relations in which he stated that if land reform were implemented in the U.S., "American farmers would fight with anything that they had to save their private property . . ." He estimates 2 million deaths if the violence were proportionate to El Salvador. "El Salvador: Agrarian reform . . ."
p. 117, bottom: "El Salvador: Agrarian reform . . ." op. cit., p. 70.
p. 119, paragraph 2: Menendez, p. 158.
p. 119, paragraph 3: Tomás Guerra, *El Salvador en La Hora de la Liberación,* (San José: Ed. Farabundo Marti), p. 166.
p. 119-120: *El Salvador Land Reform: 1980-1981, Impact Audit,* (Boston: Oxfam America, 1981), p. 70.
p. 120, paragraph 2: Martin Diskin, "Land Reform in El Salvador: An Evaluation," in *Culture and Agriculture,* issue 13, Fall 1981, p. 3.
p. 120, paragraph 3: Jay Mallin, "El Salvador's Three-Sided War: Brothers Slaughter Brothers," *Eagle,* Feb. 1981, p. 25.
p. 121, paragraph 3: *Newsweek,* March 16, 1981, p. 37.
p. 121, paragraph 4: Menendez, p. 158.
p. 121-122: Guerra, p. 171-172.
p. 123, paragraph 2: U.S. Ambassador Devine's description.

Chapter X

DEATH AND VIOLENCE

Human rights is a huge subject including what Americans call civil rights, but also social and economic rights. If you want to be thoroughly chilled and shocked, read A.J. Langguth, *Hidden Terrors* (New York:

Pantheon Books, 1978), advertised as "The truth about U.S. police operations in Latin America." A very useful comparison of Carter's and Reagan's human rights policies and beyond is Howard J. Wiarda (ed.) *Human Rights and U.S. Human Rights Policy,* (Washington: American Enterprise Institute, 1982). It's on the conservative side. "The Situation in El Salvador," hearings before the Committee on Foreign Relations, United States Senate, March 18 and April 9, 1981, on the other hand is a free-for-all of rightists, leftists, centrists, politicians, experts and so forth, all trying to give their shade of bias to the El Salvador crisis. Human rights is extensively discussed. Philippe Bourgois, a doctoral candidate in Anthropology at Stanford University on the other hand brings us up close to the human rights tragedy in his paper "What U.S. Foreign Policy Faces in Rural El Salvador: An Eyewitness Account" *Monthly Review,* vol. 34, May 1, 1982. Bourgois was trapped for 14 days with about 1,000 peasants in northern Salvador. He saw, smelled, heard and tasted what it's all about and the result is interesting. "El Salvador: 'A gross and consistent pattern of human rights' abuse,' " is the title of a small special report from Amnesty International, issued in March of 1982. A dry, but instructive book is the annual "Country Reports on Human Rights Practices" submitted to the House and Senate every year by the State Department. It covers most countries in the world. Two final books which should be read are: *Report on Human Rights in El Salvador* (New York: Vantage Books, 1982) compiled by the Americas Watch Committee and the American Civil Liberties Union, and the very impressive piece of research, Lars Schoultz's *Human Rights and United States Policy Toward Latin America,* (Princeton: Princeton University Press, 1981).

Chapter Notes

p. 132-134: This narration is translated and adapted from Guerra, op. cit. p. 46-50.

p. 134-135: The cult of death and violence in this discussion comes from the excellent book *The Mexican Cult of Death in Myth and Literature,* (Gainsville: University of Florida Press, 1976) by Barbara L.C. Brodman.

p. 136, paragraph 2: Colombian violence is described and analyzed in great detail by Germán Guzmán Campos, Orlando Fals Borda, and Eduardo Umaña Luna, *La Violencia in Colombia,* two Vols. (Bogota: Tercer Mundo, vol. I, 1963, Vol. II, 1964).

p. 137, paragraph 2: the Venezuelan case is illustrated in various documents reprinted in W. Raymond Duncan and James Nelson Goodsell, (eds.), *The Quest For Change in Latin America,* (London: Oxford University Press, 1970).

p. 137, paragraph 4: Lyman Holder, "They Shoot People, Don't They? A Look at Soviet Terrorist Mentality," *Air University Review,* Sept.-Oct., 1981, pp. 83-88.

p. 138, paragraph 4: Quoted in J. Fred Rippy, *Latin America,* (Ann Arbor: The University of Michigan Press, 1958), p. 421, Cabrera ruled from 1889-1920.

p. 139, paragraph 1: James Berry Motley, "International Terrorism: A New Mode of Warfare," *International Security Review*, Vol. VI, No. 1, 1981, pp. 93-111.
p. 139, paragraph 3: The rapes were committed by security forces ostensibly one imagines as part of the interrogation process. See Guerra, op. cit.
p. 140, paragraph 3: Jay Mallin (ed.), *"Ché" Guevara on Revolution*, (N.Y.: Dell Publishing Co., 1969), p. 30.
p. 140, paragraph 3: ibid., p. 161.
p. 141, paragraph 2: *Country Reports on Human Rights Practices*, Department of State, February 2, 1981, p. 428.
p. 141, paragraph 4: *U.S. Policy Toward El Salvador*, Congressional Hearings, March 5, 11, 1981, pp. 112-121.
p. 141, paragraph 1: These are among the conclusions drawn by Guzmán Campos, et. al., op. cit.
p. 144-145: cited in Guerra, op. cit., pp. 55-70. Translated and adapted.

Chapter XI

SACRED AND DEADLY: THE CHURCH IN EL SALVADOR

In 1970 Donald Eugene Smith published his book *Religion and Political Development*, (Boston: Little, Brown and Co., 1970). El Salvador is mentioned only twice in 298 pages, and then only because it happens to be listed with other countries. By 1983, El Salvador is the prototype of church, state, violence, suffering and revolution. Penny Lernoux's excellent *Cry of The People: The Struggle for Human Rights in Latin America – The Catholic Church in Conflict With U.S. Policy* (Harmondsworth: Penguin Books, 1982) is a chilling, frightening book, and a primer for understanding the plight of the Catholic Church today. More focused and scholarly is Lawrence Littwin, *Latin America: Catholicism and Class Conflict* (Encino: Dickenson Publishing Co., 1974), a small book with three excellent case studies of Mexico, Chile and Cuba among some theoretical material. I have already recommended Erdozain's book on Archbishop Romero and it obviously is important, but I would also read *El Salvador: El Eslabon Mas Pequeño*, (San José: EDUCA, 1980) especially Chapter 2, "Christianism and Politics." The book, written by a leader of the Frente Democrático Revolucionario and former rector of the University of El Salvador, Rafael Manjivar, juxtaposes the role of the church with revolutionary activities, pointing out that the church has often been the victim of political manipulation and cynicism.

Chapter Notes

p. 145-146: *Des Moines Register*, February 23, 1982.
p. 146, last paragraph: Webre, op. cit., p. 186.
p. 147, paragraph 1: Ivan Vallier, "Religious Elites: Differentiation and Development in Roman Catholicism," in Seymour Martin Lipset and Aldo Solari (eds.), *Elites in Latin America*, (New York: Oxford University Press 1967), p. 190.

p. 147, paragraph 2: C.H. Haring, *The Spanish Empire in America,* (New York: Harcourt, Brace and World, Inc., 1963), p. 173.

p. 147, paragraph 2: Charles Gibson, (ed.), *The Spanish Tradition in America,* (New York: Harper and Row, 1968), pp. 177-182.

p. 148, paragraph 1 and 2: cited in Lewis Hanke (ed.), *Mexico and the Caribbean,* (New York: Van Norstrand, 1967), p. 131.

p. 149, paragraph 2: Donald E. Smith, *Religion and Political Development,* (Boston: Little, Brown and Co., 1970), p. 241.

p. 149, paragraph 3: The life of Camilo Torres is interestingly analyzed in *Camilo Torres: El Cura Que Murio en las Guerrillas,* (Barcelona: Ed. Nova Terra, 1968).

p. 149, last paragraph: reprinted in Hanke, op. cit., p. 170.

p. 151: These quotations are from a mimeographed flier handed out.

p. 152, paragraph 2: Jon Sobrino, "Death and the Hope for Life," *Catholic Worker,* Sept. 1980, p. 1.

p. 154, last paragraph: Christopher Dickey, "Death as a Way of Life," *Playboy,* October 1981, p. 176-178.

p. 155-156: The letter is often reproduced and can be found in the congressional hearings on El Salvador, "U.S. Policy Toward . . ." op. cit., p. 15.

p. 158-161: Ambassador White's cable is found in the Senate hearings, "The Situation in El Salvador" op. cit., p. 185.

p. 161-162: ibid.

p. 162, last paragraph: Menendez, op. cit., p. 130.

p. 163, paragraph 1: Rafael Manjivar, *El Salvador: El Eslabon Mas Pequeño,* (San José: EDUCA, 1980), p. 47.

Chapter XII

THE DISTURBING ELECTION OF 1982

In-depth analyses of the 1982 election are still in the making so in the meantime it would be wise to study how one ought to interpret elections in El Salvador in 1982 or for that matter in 1984 when the next one is scheduled. William M. Leo Grande and Carla Anna Robbins wrote an important article titled "Oligarchs and Officers: The Crisis in El Salvador," *Foreign Affairs,* Summer, 1980. It does a nice job of surveying the political terrain. An even better job, for those who read Spanish is Mario Menendez Rodriquez's *El Salvador: Una Autentica Guerra Civil,* (San José: EDUCA, 1981). The author is a Mexican journalist who spent several months with various Salvadoran guerrilla groups and interviewed their leaders. It's quite a sobering book and one which suggests that the opposition has enormously deep organizational roots in the country. A modest little article titled "Friendly Fire" in the February 17, 1982 issue of *The New Republic* should be read because it raises intriguing questions about political tactics and elections in El Salvador.

Chapter Notes

p. 165-166, bottom & top: *The New Republic,* Feb. 17, 1982.

p. 166:   The discussion of the election of this chapter is reconstructed
from *Time, Newsweek, La Nación, The New York Times, The Christian
Science Monitor, Excélsior, El Tiempo,* and several Salvadoran newspapers.
p. 167: interviews, San José, Costa Rica.
p. 168, paragraph 3:   *Time,* March 22, 1982.
p. 168, paragraph 4:   *The Christian Science Monitor,* March 25, 1982.
p. 170, top: This document was introduced by Ambassador White at Senate hearings. See "The Situation . . ." op. cit., pp. 119-159.
p. 170, paragraph 3:   *The Christian Science Monitor,* March 15, 1982.
p. 171, top: *The Chicago Tribune,* March 3, 1982.
p. 173, paragraph 2:   I have seen a number of conflicting ballot totals
reported. See *The Economist,* April 3, 1982, p. 67; *The New York Times,*
April 2, 1982; *The Christian Science Monitor,* April 8, 1982.
p. 174, paragraph 1:   *The New York Times,* April 2, 1982, pl.
p. 174, paragraph 3:   *The Christian Science Monitor,* May 2, 1982.
p. 174, paragraphs 4 & 5:   *The New York Times,* May 2, 1982.
p. 175, paragraph 1:   *Time,* May 3, 1982.
p. 175, paragraph 2 & 3:   *La Nación,* May 3, 1982.
p. 176, paragraph 1-3:   *Time,* May 31, 1982.
p. 176, paragraph 4:   *The New York Times,* April 3, 1982.

Chapter XIII

NEW DIRECTIONS AND OLD PROBLEMS

A small book, *El Salvador: No Middle Ground,* (Chicago: New American Movement, 1981) edited by Rick Kunnes is an interesting collection of
material critical of U.S. policy; favorable to a leftist victory. For those
who read Spanish, Tomás Guerra's, *El Salvador en la Hora de la Liberación,*
(San José: Ed. Farabundo Marti, 1980) is indispensible. The book is a
veritable buffet of short pieces covering the platform and strategies of the
Salvadoran revolutionaries, U.S. policy in Central America, torture, the
military junta, Archbishop Romero's murder, land reform and so on. Most
of the pieces were short articles published by the author elsewhere. Un-
doubtedly the most stimulating reading is an article by Gabriel Zaid,
"Enemy Colleagues: A Reading of the Salvadoran Tragedy" in *Dissent,*
Winter, 1982 and the response by Phillip Berryman "Another View of El
Salvador," *Dissent,* Summer 1982 which is a very strong refutation of
Zaid's arguments. It is accompanied by a response to Berryman from Zaid.
The exchange revolves around the issue of whether the guerrillas use vio-
lence, terrorism and coercion as much as the right does (which Zaid argues
and Berryman tries to refute). A thoroughly predictable anti-American
policy book, but one which is intelligent and well executed is Robert
Armstrong and Janet Shenk, *El Salvador: The Face of Revolution,* (Boston: South End Press, 1982). Richard E. Feinberg, *Central America:
International Dimensions of the Crisis,* forthcoming 1983 from Holmes
and Meier should be an enlightening book on the regional aspects of the

situation. Robert A. Pastor's article "Our Real Interests in Central America," *The Atlantic Monthly,* July 1982 is fascinating, especially his view that the U.S. is becoming a "Caribbean" nation (mostly by immigration) and that thus American policy in the region should reflect this pending reality.

Chapter Notes

p. 179: Interview, San Salvador.

p. 182, paragraph 4 & 5: Rick Kunnes (ed.), *El Salvador: No Middle Ground,* (Chicago: New American Movement, 1981), pp. VII-X.

p. 183, paragraph 1: ibid.

p. 183, paragraph 3: interview, 1982. All the subsequent quotations are from interviews in San Salvador, Washington, D.C., Guatemala, San José, Costa Rica and several locations which if listed might compromise the anonymity of the respondents.

p. 186, paragraph 2 and 3: A substantial segment of the guerrillas are anything but Boy Scouts. See for example Gabriel Zaid, "Enemy Colleagues: A Reading of the Salvadoran Tragedy," *Dissent,* Winter, 1982, and also Leonard R. Sussman, "El Salvador is Not Just Another Zimbabwe," *The Wall Street Journal,* August 26, 1982.

p. 185, paragraph 2: Even when projects are successful the farmer and campesino are less likely than the middleman and landowner to reap the benefits as Eduardo R. Quiroga argues in "La revolución verde en el contexto institucional de Latinoamérica: Un caso de estudio en El Salvador," N/S: Volume VI, No. 12, 1981.

p. 190, paragraph 2: *Juan de Mairena,* op. cit.

INDEX

214

Human rights, (see violence)
Hungary, 189

IBM, 84
Ilopango Airport, 53
Ilopango, Lake, 3
Indians, 34, 147,
Inter-American Development Bank, 48, 91
Inter-American Human Rights Commission, 92
Iran, 124, 126
Israel, 23, 29, 171
Iturbide, Augustin de, 36, 43
Ivan the Terrible (Tzar Ivan IV), 138
Izalco, 41, 46

Japan, 48, 65
Jesuits, 6, 146
"Jesuit Mafia," 104
Jesus Christ, 152, 163
Jamaica, 24, 124
John Paul II, Pope, 145-146

Kelly, Joseph F., 89
Kennedy, Edward 166, 169, 182
Kennedy, John, 175
Kennedy, Theodore, 7
Kent State University, 25
KGB, 137
King, Martin Luther. 149
Knight, Brigadier General Albion, 25
Korea, 65
Kunnes, Rick, 182

La Cayetana, 86
La Gran Via, 33
La Libertad, 1, 159
La Maison Doreé, 32
La Nación, 175
Laos, 24
   analogy, 125
La Union, 132
Land Reform, 1, 51
Land Reform Institute (ISTA), 2, 10, 64, 118
La Violencia, (Colombia), 136, 141-142
Leiken, Robert, 27, 171
Le Monde, 25
Lemus, Col. Jose Maria, 47, 48, 49, 56, 57
Lennon, John, 3
Levantamiento, 97
Liebes, Ernesto, 93
Liewen, Edwin, 45
Ligas Populares 28 de Febrero (LP-28), 110, 123
Lion D' or, 32
London, 35
Long, Clarence, 182
López Portillo, José, 170
Los Angeles, 187
Louvain University, 149
Lozano, Ignacio, 91-92

Luna, Alfonso, 74
Libya, 124

MAG (Ministry of Agriculture), 118
Magaña, Alvaro, 174-175
Majano, Adolfo, 18, 104, 110
   endorses negotiation, 170
Malespin, Francisco, 38
Malicia, 8, 9
Mallin, Jay, 140
Managua, Nicaragua, 15
Maravilla, Jose Mario, 6
Marighela, Carlos, 140
Martell, No. 4, 33
Martell, Col. Simon Tadeo, 111
Martinez, Alvaro, 55
Martinez, Br. Boris, 6
Martinez, Maximiliano Hernández, 40-42, 56
Maryknoll, 147, 150
Maryknoll, (magazine), 162
Massie, Ian, 93
Matthew, 154
Mayorga, Román, 104, 110
McDonald, Dennis, 93
McDonald, Ronald, 80, 89-90
Medellin (Colombia), 150
Medrano, General Jose Alberto, 64, 81-82, 93, 94
Medrano, Chicas, Francisco, 5
Mejia, Colonel Benjamin, 82-83
Meléndez family, 40
Melendez, Joseph Olores, 159
Mendoza, Humberto, 6
Menendez, Francisco, 38
Menendez, Mario, 115, 162
Menendez, Rodriguez, Mario, 21, 24
Menjivar, Dr. Rafael, 83, 163
Mesa, Joel, 160
Metapán, 125
Metropolitan Cathedral, 6, 15
Mexico, 16, 34, 84, 90
   Embassy seized, 92
   Campos seeks asylum, 134
   "Cult of death," 133-135
   and political settlement, 170
Middle of the Road Government, 13
Migration, 11, 12
Military, (see specific names and events)
   anti-guerrilla war, 139, 165-166
   corruption, 88-89, 116
   coups, 1972, 82-83
   coups, 1979, 100-104
   internal cleavages, 88-89
   massacres, 15-16, 86
   political role, 45-46, 89-90
   revolts, 1932, 41-43,
   revolts, 1984, 46-47, 56
   self-analysis, 47
   "Soccer" War, 52-53
Military Academy, 104